From the *Mayflower* to
Monterrey . . . and Back

From the *Mayflower* to Monterrey . . . and Back

Two Hundred Years of Family History in the United States and Mexico

Rodrigo Quintanilla

9780578365466 (paperback)
9780578365503 (ebook)

What you leave behind is not what is engraved in stone monuments, but what is woven into the lives of others.

—Pericles

Contents

Nantucket, USA
Frederick W. Coffin
Born: 1855
Crossed border: 1880s
Marriage: 1887
Children born: 1888, 1889, 1892

Monterrey, Mexico
Rodrigo Quintanilla
Born: 1956
Crossed border: 1981
Marriage: 1984
Children born: 1989, 1992

Pedro F. Quintanilla-Coffin and Rodrigo Quintanilla

"I owe it to my grandfather to send one [of my children] back."

Pedro F. Quintanilla-Coffin
December 16, 1984
New York, New York

Preface

A few years ago, I came across this photograph that was taken in front of a partly visible Statue of Liberty in the New York City harbor. A friend from Monterrey, Mexico, took it in June 1982, when I was twenty-six years old. I was touring New York City with him. Back then, I had no idea that I was going to settle and live the rest of my adult life in the New York City area. Many years later, while commuting to my job in lower Manhattan along this same route during 2006 and 2007, I got the idea to write a narrative about my search for information about my great-grandfather Frederick W. Coffin and his family. He was born in Nantucket, Massachusetts, but his life ended in Mexico. My siblings and I grew up knowing very little about this man, and I was playing catch-up to learn more about his life. Ironically, the Statue of Liberty was dedicated in 1886, and my great-grandfather never saw it because he was living in Mexico.

Rodrigo Quintanilla, New York City Harbor, June 1982

This book encompasses more than thirty years of research, largely concentrated during the past fifteen years. I focused at first on a single individual in my family tree, but my endless curiosity broadened my research to include several generations and family branches in two countries, starting when European settlers first stepped foot in the New World. As soon as I found the answer to one question, other questions popped up. However, the narrative itself centers on the early 1800s, when the United States was a young and small nation, and concludes in Mexico as the new millennium approached.

My formal research for information on the Coffin family began in September 1981, when I arrived at the University of Pennsylvania in Philadelphia to pursue graduate studies. There was a void in our knowledge about our links to the United States when I was growing up in Mexico. My father attempted to learn more about his North American roots but without much success. For me, living in the United States led to a renewed need to learn about both my North American and my Mexican ancestries, building upon my father's initial scarce (and often inaccurate) knowledge.

Oral history sometimes complements family stories, yet this was not my case. For some unexplained reason, no one in the family ever spoke about my great-grandfather Frederick. It was almost as if he had never existed. Slowly, my research brought back to life not only Frederick but also his parents and his grandparents as well as individuals from other family branches. There have been so many layers to this research. My search for information on Frederick technically ended on October 28, 2015, when I located his elusive death certificate in the state of Durango in Mexico. This journey had been long indeed but incredibly rewarding. I learned so much more about many other ancestors. As I slowly dug into my North American lineage, my curiosity naturally expanded into the Quintanilla lineage in Mexico and how Frederick's life connected to it.

One interesting point is that women keep their names from birth to death in the Spanish tradition. Therefore, it is much easier to follow records using their birth names throughout their life events in Mexico. In contrast, women in the United States usually change their names once married, making it more difficult to find records during their life span should you not know who they married and how their legal names changed. This gets only more complicated if they marry more than once and surnames change accordingly.

Genealogy research has become less cumbersome today compared to those distant days when my research efforts first started. There are many more tools readily available to genealogy researchers. The Church of Jesus Christ of Latter-day Saints database has been the main source for the information I have gathered. I complemented missing information with that of Ancestry.com. Small steps at times, gigantic leaps at others, and a fair number of lucky breaks

Frederick W. Coffin, Northern Mexico, ca. 1890

expanded this genealogical research into a more complete family history over time. I got extremely excited when I found a new ancestor who I could bring back to life. And it was even more exciting when I uncovered unknown facts, such as missing children, second or third marriages, and sometimes the cause of death.

This narrative focuses on families formed in the early 1800s and the individual who connected them—Frederick W. Coffin. I also provide direct lines of descent dating back to the 1620s (US) and 1500s (Mexico), but I placed these in the two appendices at the end to avoid clutter. I have answered a few important questions about this individual, but many others remain unanswered. Although I am still not completely certain about what motivated him, learning about his family and upbringing allows me to have a window into his character and the traits that drove his behavior.

Finding information about him has truly been an enriching journey. Contrary to what I previously believed, he did not live in Monterrey for an extended period. Instead, he resided most often in the mining locations of Coahuila and Durango along the new railroad lines being laid in the country. From the information I do have, I know he worked for a newly formed railroad company and resided in San Luis Potosí for some time.

I hope readers will be encouraged to find more about their own families and ancestry after I share this narrative. In researching these families, we need to keep in mind that most of these individuals have been dead for many years—nothing of their world remains, and no one who knew them well is alive today. Some benefit from ample records left also in last wills, land grants, or disputes. These individuals have come to life again as I wrote about their families and experiences, a privilege reserved only for those who achieved long-lasting fame. But, at the end of the day, as Marcus Tullius Cicero once noted: "The life of the dead is placed in the memory of the living." We only hope our memory and findings do them justice.

Introduction

Our earliest memories are usually of our parents. Perhaps we remember how they held our hands when we walked and went places. Their hands touched our faces and our hair, and ours touched theirs. Babies spend countless hours examining their hands when they are a few months old. As we grow older and have children of our own, we in turn hold their hands and touch their hair and faces too. And when we look at our hands, we can envision how our grandparents touched us and their grandparents touched them as well. I am fortunate today to hold my granddaughter's hand and picture how symbolically my grandparents are reaching out to her through me. And then I think that one day, hopefully, she will hold her own grandchildren's hands, and I, too, may be reaching out to them, even when I am no longer here. For me, hands thus become the vessel that moves across generations. So, for me, hands become how generations meet across time.

Life is constantly shifting, even if at times those changes seem imperceptible, and the ticktock of clocks seems foolishly unhurried. Families are truly in perpetual motion, being disassembled and rearranged, with individuals dying and new ones being born or joining in through marriage. Older families eventually dissolve, and new families are formed, and eventually these, too, ultimately fall apart and come to an end, like most everything else. Nothing is permanent.

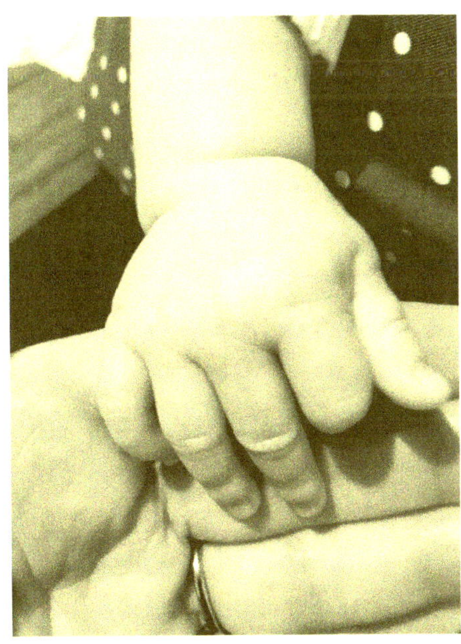

Rodrigo Quintanilla holding granddaughter Esme's hand

Wedding photographs show the beginning of a new family. Both bride and groom gaze into the future, hoping for a happy and promising life ahead. Moments are forever frozen, locking a couple's optimism for what may be heading their way. Neither one of them contemplates potential disappointments, regrets, or hurt in those snapshots that suspend such a fleeting moment in their lives. If asked, I am certain these couples would say that they will be happy to deal with whatever struggles and challenges they might find on the road ahead, in illness or in health.

Family portraits follow wedding pictures as children join in, which also show their parents' pride. Spouses and grandchildren are added down the line. To be sure, most parents think only of giving their children the best possible future, providing them with loving homes and seeking opportunities that may lead to a successful and happy life ahead. These children later form their own families, passing on values learned from their parents to their children, and so on. But with every new generation, family ties and knowledge are eventually lost and deceased relatives forgotten.

And then there are those shameful family secrets. At their best, they are uncomfortable moments, sometimes funny with the benefit of hindsight but mostly not. Some events, however, truly haunt family members. They are too appalling or embarrassing to be discussed in public, and it is best if they are entirely forgotten and never spoken of ever again. Typically, these secrets relate to the black sheep in the family. We all have those in our families, and every generation seems to count at least one.

To be sure, family stories have a lot of joy but also a lot of sorrow. The travails of ordinary daily life sooner or later mold families' lives because the politics, the geographic dislocation, and the economics of their day place many constraints. Some are lucky to remain in place across generations despite the challenges they face. For others, living conditions become so tough that they are forced to seek new opportunities elsewhere. Throughout their lives, these families enjoy both cheerful and heartbreaking events and undoubtedly encounter challenges in getting through whatever they face. And as I now see photographs of my children, I imagine that they, too, will have their own dreams to follow one day and goals to achieve for their newly formed families.

The dissolution of the core family unit once one parent dies, especially when children are young and perhaps still unmarried, is a common thread. Sometimes this dissolution is quick and unforgiving. Other times it might take several years, yet it is nonetheless very painful. Moreover, in every generation, there are those who die young, who never get to finish their lives. Who knows what their legacy and contributions would have been had they fulfilled their own potential.

Reading last wills has been enlightening too. Decedents put such care into how they want their estates and prized personal possessions distributed. There is always the principle of equality, even if there is no agreement as to its definition. There are lapel pins, earrings, rings, silver spoons or sets, writing desks, paintings, and so on. All very important to the testator. But what happened to all those prized possessions over time? Were they kept within the family? Do descendants know or even care about the importance these items held for their original owner? The answers are probably negative. And within a few generations, those prized possessions often disappear.

Last, women in these societies and throughout all these generations had no real choices available to them other than marriage. A young woman from those eras could look forward to very narrow options in life. For the most part, only a husband could provide financial support and social standing. It was typically through marriage that these women acquired wealth and secured their social position, unless they inherited it directly from their side of the family. Many felt they needed to secure a second husband if their first one died prematurely. Moreover, many were not allowed to own property in their name. And it was difficult for women to escape physical or any type of abuse in those unfortunate cases when it existed.

Men, on the other hand, seem to have pursued second or even third marriages to ensure that their dynasty and name survived through the years when a young wife died, especially in childbirth. Wives were considered important caregivers. Children—numerous children—were needed to counter high mortality rates.

In the chapters that follow, we focus on the one individual who linked two families through time—Frederick William Coffin. The locations where these families lived have changed throughout the centuries. The early settlers of Massachusetts came in search of religious freedom. Their relationship with native people was complicated, to say the least. In time, both New Bedford and Nantucket grew to have thriving communities in the 1800s located in what became the wealthiest and most densely populated region of the young United States.

In contrast, the northeast region of Mexico was dusty and desertlike. It was isolated from the economic and political power of Mexico City. The typical Spanish settlers of the sixteenth and seventeenth centuries were either missionaries or adventurers who sought riches in mining, land grants, and human exploitation. Many enslaved natives for their economic benefit. Most were also looking for religious freedom but not the same kind as those in Massachusetts. They were crypto-Jews[1] or "new" Christians who desired to practice

---

1. This refers to the secret adherence to Judaism while publicly professing the Catholic faith.

their ancient rituals without the meticulous oversight of the Catholic Church and the government. The long distance from Mexico City and Spain offered a certain level of religious protection from the Inquisition. Many practiced their traditional Jewish rituals in hiding.[2]

Moreover, Monterrey and its surrounding area lacked a significant indigenous population to exploit, and mining opportunities were limited. Nomadic and aggressive indigenous peoples sparsely populated the region, and the soil was not particularly suitable for farming. The agriculture that did exist supported mining towns in Central Mexico. Water was also scarce. Many native people became enslaved, as did people brought from Africa, to provide free labor under the excuse of saving their souls through religious conversion. These lands would not produce sustainable and wide-ranging wealth for a long time.

Despite obvious differences, both Spanish and English settlers of these different geographies shared common traits: their strength in character, their hardiness, and their resilience in overcoming adverse living conditions and unwelcoming native peoples. During these past two hundred years, there has been a reversal of fortunes of sorts as well. New Bedford and many New England towns have suffered from a steady economic decline, while Monterrey has become Mexico's third-largest city and an industrial behemoth that provides wealth to many of its residents and the rest of the country.

The chapters that follow will show how these families evolved during the past two hundred years.

---

2. Much has been written about the crypto-Jews settling in the north of Mexico in the sixteenth and seventeenth centuries.

A Void to Fill

I realized the significant void that existed around my father's life in 1976 when we visited the island of Nantucket, off the coast of Massachusetts. His grandfather was born on the island, and family connections were lost after his death. We were his first descendants from Mexico to set foot on the island. Others followed over time, but this was a very special first trip. My father had a profound sense of family, lineage, and heritage. He was proud of who he was and of all those who had preceded him in life. Yet his grandfather Frederick was absent from this lineage.

My father was a man of his generation in every respect. Born in 1914 during a tumultuous time in Mexico, his was an age when elders were respected without question—when tradition, proper manners, and integrity made up the fabric of everyday life. He entered adulthood in the 1930s, during the global Depression years, just as Mexico itself was leaving a time of political and social upheaval to enjoy some economic and political stability. The army support of presidents ended with the election of the first civilian in 1940.

My father developed an intense and long-lasting love for the city in which he lived most of his life, and he was never comfortable to leave it for long. And those times when he did, he always missed it, happy to return to familiar surroundings.

He epitomized those individuals who are content to live all their lives in one place. Individuals happy to give back all they can to

Pedro F. Quintanilla-Coffin, ca. 1939

the land that nourished their body and soul, trying to make it a better place for all to enjoy. Until the end of his days, he always referred to Monterrey as his home.

To others, our birthplace is merely an accident of nature and might be too confining. The entire world offers exciting opportunities for exploration and excitement too enriching to pass over. These people are restless by nature; they prefer to be like a feather drifting in the wind, pleased to set foot in random places, eager to embrace new experiences, people, and customs, ready for adventure. That, I came to believe, was my father's grandfather—Frederick W. Coffin.

From the time I was a young adolescent, I tried to imagine living far away from home. "What sort of places, people, and life existed beyond my city's beautiful mountains?" I asked myself during those lazy, warm, and sun-filled afternoons in Monterrey, alone at home and unbothered because most of my siblings had already left our parents' home. My mother would often try to reassure herself that I would never leave, but I never had the heart to tell her that my soul was impatient for all that lay ahead for me in some distant place. I, too, loved the city I was born in. Still, I left Monterrey when I graduated from college in June 1977 and have not returned since but for very brief visits. Nonetheless, the city runs deep in my veins, with memories, mine and those of my ancestors, embedded deeply in my soul. Like many young children, I enjoyed listening to family stories and learning about different relatives. Everything was confusing, because my father's side of the family was large or because my mother's family hailed from different geographies. Memories and anecdotes were passed on to keep alive most of those who had already died.

But even among all these relatives, deep mystery surrounded one individual in particular—my great-grandfather Frederick W. Coffin, or Federico, as my family called him. Who was this man? All about him was obscure and enigmatic. Family conversations seldom included him. No one in the family was named after him, which was unusual for a country like Mexico. When questions did arise, they were mostly brushed off and left unanswered. I am sure whatever little firsthand information there was about him was lost as people who knew him began to pass away.

Rodrigo Quintanilla, Monterrey, May 1977

I suspect that Frederick Coffin probably felt restless, too, but in his case, mountains did not confine his dreams. Instead, I imagine the blue, cold waters that surround Nantucket Island controlled his thrill for adventure or aspiration for fortune. Those waters offer a perilous and formidable physical obstacle even today. He must have been impatient to leave his place of birth as remote locations beckoned. The immediate years after the Civil War offered only a moribund local economy and poor financial prospects on the island to young Frederick.

My father's sense of belonging and family came out loud and clear on November 2, the Day of the Dead in Mexico. While North Americans usually avoid the topic of death, Mexicans revere deceased ancestors and make every effort to remember them. In fact, a person never dies if we keep their name alive. Our family, however, were "modern urbanite" Mexicans, so we did not follow traditional Day of the Dead festivities, which included all family members gathering at the cemetery for gravesite reunions more festive than somber. These types of celebrations are more common in Central Mexico. We did not bring along picnic baskets, bottles of tequila for toasting the departed, or a mariachi band to lead a heartfelt sing-along.

My father took my brothers and me to the cemetery to honor our departed in a quiet, reverent way. We brought flowers. We visited the graves of his parents, grandparents, and many other relatives during those gray, cool, autumn Monterrey afternoons. He led us from plot to plot, perhaps thinking of many memories that he could not share with us because we simply were too young and removed to appreciate them.

And although some graves did have the unusual Coffin surname combined with Spanish ones inscribed on them, one name was always absent—that of Frederick W. Coffin. We seldom spoke about him during those long walks among the tombstones.

As I grew up and learned the names of these relatives, I examined their gravestones and imagined what their lives might have been like. I could sometimes relate a name to an old and faded

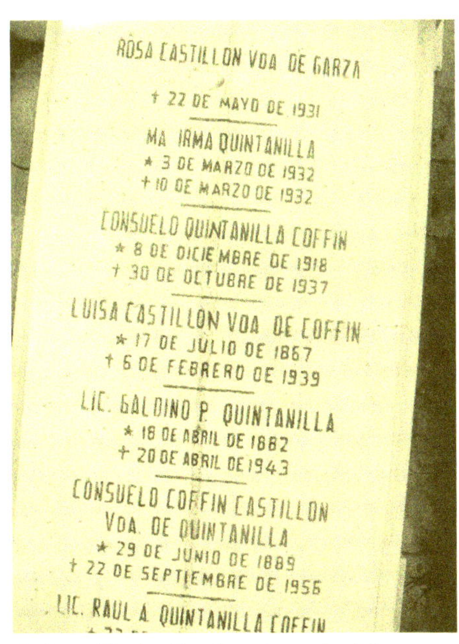

Quintanilla family plot, Panteón del Carmen

photograph. To these visits, my brothers and I could add the few dinner stories and anecdotes we heard from my mother, even if these were not her blood relatives, but less so from my father. We had many more stories from my mother's side, to which her parents would often add some color at family gatherings. Sadly, the only grandparents I had known had passed away, too, by my midteens, and with them many of their stories. Unfortunately, I was too young to ask the right questions then.

With age, I have come to have a different appreciation for cemeteries. Until fairly recently, to me, these were just solitary, ignored places. Today I think of that time when a body is laid to rest and close relatives weep for the loss of their loved ones amid intense grief. As Harriet Beecher Stowe famously noted, "The bitterest tears shed over graves are for words left unsaid and deeds left undone." I think of the many times that the living come to visit with quiet tears and regret. And although good memories may undoubtedly abound, I think that there may also be bad memories of remorse for misdeeds done unto them, hurtful words uttered to or by them, and regret for the forgiveness not given or asked for. At the very least, there is a lament for the time and opportunities lost.

Slowly, I began to notice some coincidences between Frederick Coffin's life and mine. This was a man who left everything he knew and the only family he had for adventure and fortune in a faraway place. He may have had no choice, given the economic circumstances he was living in, but he must have been adventurous nonetheless to end up in Mexico in the 1880s. He traveled long distances, to a remote place, and settled in a country where sentiment toward the United States was raw from a recent war in which Mexico lost half of its territory.

For all the complexities of this period, however, he appears to have been quick to respond to the shifting winds of the world around him, and he wasted no time seeking riches in something new: talk in Nantucket of fresh discoveries of gold and silver in California likely beckoned. He ultimately settled down within a culture that was completely different from his own and with a language in which he was not completely fluent. Geographically speaking, he could not have chosen another place less like Nantucket than Northern Mexico. Yet from what we can tell, he fully embraced this new life and adopted its culture and customs. And as quickly as he appeared, he was gone. He died young by today's standards, probably alone, suddenly, and perhaps even dispirited, far from the people who knew him from childhood. Far from the land that he had once loved.

Like him, when I was young, I passionately wanted to leave my hometown and experience what the wider world had to offer. In an almost imperceptible way, my life began to mirror his when I first set foot on Nantucket in 1976.

Frederick W. Coffin, Northern Mexico, ca. 1890

I, like him, left my country, my culture, my language, my family, and my friends. I soon realized that I was born nearly a hundred years after him, and I, too, married a woman from my adopted country who did not share my faith, language, or culture, and I settled far from my place of birth. My children were born exactly one hundred years after Frederick's. Yet, unlike him, I survived the turn of the century, and as I ultimately discovered, our lives have been quite different.

The Search Begins

In 1976, my parents and I traveled for the first time to Nantucket when one of my brothers was pursuing a graduate degree at Brown University. Unbeknownst to us at that time, Brown University had a special significance for the Coffin family. Frederick's grandfather Timothy G. Coffin had enrolled there in 1809 and graduated in 1813. Rufus, Frederick's father, attended the college from 1835 to 1837, but the school dismissed him that year for undisclosed reasons.

We did not know then of Nantucket's popularity as a summer retreat, nor did we realize that the island pretty much shut down to nonresidents during the off-season. It was during this trip that I first saw the old photographs and illustrations of our North American ancestors that my father carried to show to newly found relatives. I recall the portrait of his great-grandfather Rufus Coffin, some photo-graphs of Frederick, a picture of his young sister, and a couple of photographs of a house with at least one woman standing on the porch. From Providence, Rhode Island, we drove to Woods Hole, Massachusetts, to take the ferry to Nantucket one chilly evening that March. This felt like we were traveling back in time, landing in a very quaint yet extremely unfamiliar New England town.

This was the first time that anyone in our family had ventured so far north into the United States. Up to this point, I could not fathom a cold beach with pine and other evergreen trees. The beaches I knew were sunny and warm and had palm trees. It was a total culture shock. Just as North Americans find Mexico kind of backward, we Northern Mexicans were used to the developed, open-spaced, and orderly appearance of the US border states. Nantucket lacked flashy hotels, shopping malls, or dining places, especially back in 1976. There were old cobblestoned streets, quaint wooden dwellings, and small church steeples on deserted streets that chilly March.

Upon arrival in Nantucket, we were lucky to find a bed-and-breakfast that would take us for our short stay. We were also lucky to find somewhere to dine that frigid evening. After failed attempts to locate a suitable place to eat

Rodrigo Quintanilla, the coast off Cape Cod,
March 1976

at 10:00 p.m., our dinner was snacks and sodas from the 7-Eleven store close
to the docks. That evening, as we settled down for the night, my father jok-
ingly told my mother that his grandfather knew we had come to Nantucket
and that he would visit us that night. The following morning, he claimed that
he did hear a knock on the door as we all fell asleep, but that when he opened
it, he found nobody there.

Our first day in Nantucket was one of exploration and research. We
searched for genealogical records at the library of the Peter Folger Museum
(now the Nantucket Historical Association, or NHA). When the head librarian learned about our quest, he took out the book of genealogical records[3]
where we could see listed in elegant calligraphy the names of Frederick's parents, their marriage, and their four children: Frederick, Rufus Jr., Anna M.,
and Betsey P. (see copy below). We all had mixed feelings. Genuine disap-
pointment followed the initial elation. Slowly, Frederick Coffin and his family were coming back to life, the dates becoming clearer. These names were
of real people, and our knowledge had begun to expand. It was then that we
learned that Frederick was born in 1855, a few years before the Civil War
would tear the United States apart.

3. This is the original of Eliza Starbuck Barney's journal that was used for the genealogical
records in Louis Coffin, ed., *The Coffin Family* (Nantucket: Nantucket Historical Association,
1962).

Annie Mitchell Coffin, Nantucket, ca. 1870

This was only a tease. We yearned for more information. We were saddened to read that both sisters had death records next to their birthdates, indicating that they had died rather young. Rufus Jr. had no entry next to his birthdate, so we could not find a quick follow-up about him or any possible descendants. But Frederick's name had the following entry penned in ink that suggested someone had entered it at a later date: "Married Louisa [*sic*] Castillon in Monterey, Mexico in 1887." What an exciting moment of discovery!

It was clear that Frederick had communicated with his family about his new wife. My father did not speak English, but he clearly understood the entry he was reading with his grandmother's name. My father's eyes swelled with tears, evidently moved by what nobody else in his family had ever seen. Up to this point, my father knew only of Frederick's sister Annie because of an old drawing he had brought with him on this trip but not of the younger

Meeting at the Jared Coffin House in Nantucket with
Mrs. Isabel Duffy, March 1976

sister, Betsey (Bessie), nor that both these girls had died so young. There was a death entry only for Frederick's father, Rufus, but none for his mother, Winnifred, known in the family as Winnie. So many questions still remained unanswered. It was clear that the search for Coffin relatives had reached a dead end for now, since there was no way we could trace Rufus Jr.'s descendants, if they existed.

At this point, the librarian suggested we speak to Mrs. Isabel Worth Duffy, who was an expert on the history of the island and its people. On short notice, we called her and arranged for a meeting at the Jared Coffin House[4] (above) for later that same morning. This meeting with her, however, yielded no additional information. We had purchased the Coffin family book[5] back at the library, and I had identified that page 306 contained the last entry for Frederick W. Coffin—without the details about his new wife in Mexico. Aside from a pleasant exchange, there was not much more Mrs. Duffy could add. Therefore, my father resigned himself to the fact that there were no Coffin

4. Jared Coffin, not a relative, was one of the most successful shipowners during the prime whaling days. He built this mansion in 1845 in downtown Nantucket, and today it is a hotel.
5. Louis Coffin, *The Coffin Family*.

Civil War Monument, Nantucket

relatives for him to meet on this first trip. Still, his friendship with Mrs. Duffy continued until her death a few years later.

With no more leads to follow, we decided to explore the island for what it was, with no other expectations. My father felt right at home and enjoyed the island's atmosphere tremendously. As we walked up the prestigious Main Street, we discovered Frederick's father's name, Rufus Coffin, carved into one of the granite sides of the Civil War Monument. The town erected this obelisk in 1874. It bears the names of the seventy-three Nantucket men, soldiers and sailors, who lost their lives in the Civil War. It is also Nantucket's largest public monument.[6]

I think back to its dedication ceremony and how Rufus's close family and friends, including Frederick; his mother, Winnie; and his brother, Rufus, may have been present. We were unaware at that time that we had walked right past Frederick's last home on Nantucket at 69 Main Street, the original Frederick W. Mitchell house, the home of his grandmother's second husband.

We drove around the island and stumbled upon the Jethro Coffin House, the oldest residence on Nantucket. According to the Nantucket Historical Association, their parents built it in 1686 as a wedding gift for Jethro Coffin, then twenty-three, and Mary Gardner, aged sixteen. It is the sole surviving structure from the island's original seventeenth-century English settlement. Jethro Coffin (not a direct ancestor), who is listed as a blacksmith at the time of his death in 1727, was the grandson of one of the island's first white settlers and original proprietors, Tristram Coffin.

The Coffin family reunion of 1881 led to renewed interest in the preservation and restoration of the structure after this dwelling had been abandoned for quite some time. The Nantucket Historical Association acquired the house in 1923 and led its subsequent restorations. Nobody was around to let us in, and

---

6. The most complete description and the roster is included in Richard F. Miller and Robert F. Mooney, *The Civil War: The Nantucket Experience* (Pittsburgh: Wesco, 1994).

Pedro F. Quintanilla and Maria Josefina Gomez at the
Jethro Coffin House

the place was pretty much deserted because it was the off-season, but somehow
we did go in—perhaps a library staff member allowed it? Not much to see
then, but my father still loved the house and the grounds on which it was built.
So much "Coffin" around truly excited him. He had grown up with none back
in Monterrey. And thus, empty-
handed and disillusioned because
there were no leads to pursue, we
left Nantucket. On our way back
to Providence, we drove through
New Bedford, not realizing how
important that city had also been
to the Coffin family.

My father pursued the weak
Nantucket connection he found
upon our return to Mexico. He
remained in contact with Mrs.
Duffy until her death and wrote
the Nantucket Historical Association about the Coffin descendants
his grandfather had left behind in
Mexico. He was proud indeed!

Rodrigo Quintanilla, Nantucket 1976, with
the Coffin family book

Lic. Pedro F. Quintanilla Coffin
Ave. Morelos 652 Ote.
Monterrey, N.L. Mexico

                                        Providence. R. I.
                                        12 April 1976

Mrs. Isabel W. Duffy
3 Lovel Place
Nantucket, Mass.

Dear Mrs. Duffy:

My impressions of Nantucket will be written in an editorial which will
be published on my return to México in the "Diario de Monterrey", one
of the five newspapers that are most important in that mexican city.

I have colaborated in it since its foundation. To my work as a lawyer, I add that of a writer.

As a homage to such a lovely place, I would like to see it published
in the Nantucket gazzette, "Yesterday's Island".

I am sending it to you, translated by my wife and sons, as I could
not find the address of J. Richard Daub in a copy of the gazzette
that was given to me at the Jared Coffin House. I would be very
grateful if you would see to it that it is published.

                                        Affectionately yours,

                                        Pedro F. Quintanilla Coffin

'Enclosure

My father published an article about this trip in the *Diario de Monterrey* in Spanish on April 10, 1976—"Only One Hundred Years":

> I last saw you one hundred years ago, I came back Band found you unchanged. I remembered you like in a dream, in which both people and things move among clouds and foam. I saw myself running through your paths, jumping over fences and stockades, going down to the sea so that I could sit on your beaches awaiting the whaling ships, which would bring good tidings of a successful hunt or bitter news of those who would never come back.

I listened to your church bells toll slowly in the passing hours, as they used to do before they stopped time in hopes of my return. The music of your bells was a lullaby and a herald of hope, reminding your children to lift their eyes, as always done by our people, comforting their spirit and hardening their hands. Ready today for tomorrow's tasks, content with having accomplished those of yesterday. In the darkness of night, I walked again in silence along your streets and parks, and I found them cozy and heartwarming. Looking through the lit windows of your dwellings, we saw ourselves again gathered around tables warmed by loving hearths.

You made me confess, without rushing or blushing, the motives for my absence, the reasons why I left you for so long and made me promise not to do so again. And I slept peacefully, again in my home, as if I had never been gone, sheltered by your aged trees, keepers of your secrets and witnesses of your anguishes, of your beliefs and your joys. You were not too hard with your absent son but instead filled him with peace so that he could enjoy his slumber. If anything, you whispered the news of his return and your wishes to retain me, transforming the sea's fury into whispers and soft admonishment.

Again, I shook friendly hands and saw the faces of my people after an absence of one hundred years. I thank you for holding down the clock's hands for such a long time as you awaited my return to my home. And while I return once again, I leave you, Nantucket, my own forever imprisoned soul, as a reflection of my mother's eyes on your blue and brave New England waters.[7]

As the 1970s drew to their end, important events occurred in rapid succession and reshuffled my own family. In April 1979, my mother passed away suddenly. In July, the governor of the state appointed my father state attorney general. In September, his political party selected him to run for

---

7. Original published text: "*Solo dejé de verte cien años, volví, y te encontré igual. Te recordaba como en un sueño, en donde los personajes y las cosas se mueven entre nubes y espuma. Me veía correr por tus veredas, brincando cer-cas y vallados, bajando al mar, para sentarme en tus playas en espera del buque ballenero, con las buenas nuevas de la cacería feliz o con las malas de quienes ya no volvieron. Volví a oir las campanas de tu iglesia, dejando caer las horas lentamente, como lo hacían antes de detener el tiempo esperando mi regreso. La música de tu carrillón era arrullo y esperanza, recordando a tus hijos volver la vista a lo Alto, como lo hicieron siempre confortando su espíritu y endureciendo sus manos. Listos hoy para la tarea de mañana, contentos de haber cumplido con la de ayer. Volví, en la obscuridad de la noche, a caminar en silencio por tus calles y tus plazas, y las encontré tranqui-las y acogedoras. Por las luces de las ventanas de tus casas, volvimos a vernos reunidos a la mesa al amor del fuego. Me hiciste confesar, sin prisas ni rubores, los motivos de mi ausencia, las causas de haberte dejado tanto tiempo, y mis promesas de no volverlo a hacer. Y dormí tranquilo, de nuevo en mi hogar, como si nunca hubiera estado lejos, cobijado por tus viejos y añosos árboles, sabedores de tus secretos y testigos de tus angustias, de tu fé y tus alegrías. No te mostraste dura con el hijo ausente, sino lo llenaste de paz para conciliar el sueño. Si acaso, comentaste en voz baja la noticia del regreso y los deseos de retenerme, transformando la furia del mar en quedos murmullos y suaves reproches. Volví a estrechar manos amigas y volví a ver las caras de los míos después de una ausencia de solo cien años. Gracias te doy por haber detenido por tanto tiempo las manecillas de tu reloj, en es-pera de mi vuelta al hogar. Y mientras regreso de nuevo, te dejo, Nantucket, mi propia alma, aprisionada para siempre, como reflejo de los ojos de mi madre en tus aguas azules y bravas de Nueva Inglaterra.*"

mayor of the city. He was elected mayor the following month, and he took office on January 1, 1980. Upon losing my mother, what he wanted most was to have family around him, including Coffin relatives, at his inauguration.

He invited Mrs. Duffy to his inauguration, but given her age, she did not feel fit to travel such a long journey, and thus she suggested that a "young" couple from Nantucket should do so: Richard and Grace Coffin. The couple was in their sixties, but to a much older Mrs. Duffy, they were young. Although they were not related to us, they were an instant sensation with family and friends in Monterrey. Richard resembled Pope John Paul II and Grace Prime Minister Margaret Thatcher! This new friendship led to our second visit to Nantucket in the spring of 1981.

My father, now a widower, my brother Jorge, my sister Jo, and I traveled to Nantucket, some of us for the second time. It would be my father's last visit to the island. Graciously, the Coffins set us up in one of the three brick houses[8] on Main Street and offered a cocktail reception in our honor. We last saw the Coffins at my wedding on December 16, 1984, in New York City, but we exchanged Christmas cards for many years after that. Sadly, Richard Coffin passed away on April 6, 2003, and the town of Nantucket dedicated its *Annual Report for Fiscal 2002–03* to his memory.

Shortly thereafter, in the fall of 1981, I moved to Philadelphia to pursue a graduate degree at the University of Pennsylvania. When I needed a respite from studying, I would conduct searches on Rufus Coffin at the Van Pelt Library. No internet at that time! I did find a collection of Civil War writings: *The War of the Rebellion—A Compilation of the Official Records of the Union and Confederate Armies*. In it, I found records of correspondence of Lt. Rufus Coffin to his superiors.

In the years that followed, I located tidbits of information here and there that I shared with my father to continue to put the pieces together. My father passed away in November 1992. I not only felt that I needed to continue the search for Frederick on my own, but also I began to realize that my life held some parallels to his. Thirteen years would pass, however, before Frederick Coffin's name would come up again in a meaningful way.

---

8. In 1836, Joseph Starbuck hired master mason Christopher Capen to build three brick homes for his three sons, William, Mat-thew, and George. Starbuck was one of Nantucket's most prominent nineteenth-century whale oil merchants, counting among his seafaring assets *President, Hero, Omega, Three Brothers, Loper, and Young Hero*. These ships made over fifty voyages, bringing back more than eighty thousand barrels of oil valued at an estimated $2.5 million. An oil baron of his day, Starbuck could easily lavish his wealth on his three sons; he did so by building them three identical and elaborate houses on Main Street. See Will Gardner, *Three Bricks and Three Brothers* (Cambridge: Riverside Press, 1958).

Maria Josefina Quintanilla, Bernie Coffin, Grace Coffin, Mayor Pedro F. Quintanilla-Coffin, Richard Coffin,Rodrigo Quintanilla, Nantucket, spring 1981

A Renewed Focus

"Hello?" my wife, Vivian, said when she answered the telephone that May afternoon in 2005.

"I am looking for Rodrigo Quintanilla," a woman's voice said on the other end. "This is Nancy Fowler. I believe that my husband's mother was related to his great-grandfather Frederick Coffin."

I gasped in disbelief when Vivian related that call to me. My father had searched for so long for his Coffin relatives that I had given up hope. I could not believe it! As it turned out, Nancy Fowler was married to Fred Fowler Jr., grandson of Rufus Coffin Jr. (1857–1924), Frederick's brother.

The search that my father started in 1976 was coming to an end. Or was it being reignited?

Late one night in January 2002, I posted an entry in the Coffin genealogy forum in search of descendants of Rufus Coffin (Sr.). In truth, I searched for descendants of Rufus Jr., because both of my great-grandfathers' sisters died young. All we knew was that Rufus Jr. had enlisted in the US Navy and fought in the Spanish-American War (1898). Nancy Fowler slowly began to fill in some of the blanks I had. And more Mexican connections eerily appeared.

From Nancy, we learned that Rufus Jr. had resided in Boston and married Amy Wentworth Ingraham (1881–1932) in July 1910 when he was fifty-three years old and Amy only twenty-nine, two years before his niece (my grandmother) in Mexico herself married. Amy had been born in Portland, Maine. In a strange coincidence, President Buchanan appointed her father, George T. Ingraham, consul to Mexico in 1858. Rufus Jr. and Amy settled in Brookline, Massachusetts, and had two daughters in quick succession: Winifred, born in 1912, and Priscilla, born in 1913. Rufus became a bond broker and died in 1924 at the age of sixty-seven. His wife, Amy, survived him eight more years and passed away in 1932 at age fifty. Both daughters were orphaned relatively young. That same year, Priscilla married Fred Fowler Sr. Her sister, Winifred, married Edmund Colgan, an artist, in 1940. Winifred passed away in 1996 at age eighty-three, Priscilla in 1986 at age seventy-two. Ed Colgan died in 1965 at age fifty-two. Fred Fowler Sr. passed away on December 13, 2005, at the age of 101.

We soon learned that Rufus Jr. had joined the Sons of the American Revolution in 1894 through a connection with his great-great-grandfather Shadrach Standish, a descendant of Myles Standish and father of Frederick's great-grandmother Averick Standish Parker. Wait. A Standish in this lineage? A *Mayflower* voyager and signer of the Mayflower Compact?

It took another year for me to meet the descendants of Rufus Jr., when they gathered for a memorial service for Frederick Fowler Sr. in May 2006. In a strange twist of events, Frederick Fowler Sr. was born in Mexico City in 1904, the son of American missionaries and one of thirteen children. He left Mexico with his family as a teenager at the onset of the Mexican Revolution (1910–1917), but his family's ties to Mexico remained strong. My daughter, Daniela, then fourteen, and I drove up to Grantham, New Hampshire, for the memorial service and the Fowler family reunion. My heart was full of anticipation, and thoughts raced through my mind in search of any information I could learn about my great-grandfather. I was the first of the Mexican line of descendants of Rufus Coffin to contact his North American descendants in more than one hundred years.

We had a warm reception. Despite family members coming together on a sad occasion, they celebrated the life of their patriarch. As for me, I looked around to find family resemblances, and there were plenty. In particular, Richard Fowler, my father's second cousin, bore a strong resemblance to my father.

Nancy Fowler not only helped me fill in the gaps left by the many years without contact between the descendants of both brothers but also she was instrumental in facilitating a greater understanding of my great-grandfather's important lineage. We had never heard stories of ancestors linked to the *Mayflower*. I dug further to find that Rufus Coffin had not one ancestor from the *Mayflower* but nine! And a patriot from the American Revolution as well.

But I also received a key piece to the puzzle that day—at least, that is what I then believed. Before our departure, Susan Apsey, one of my father's second cousins, graciously whispered that there was something she wanted to show me that would connect me to my great-grandfather. She walked me to a book-case and took out an old family Bible. Her mother, Annie Mitchell, presented this Bible to Rufus and Winnifred Coffin upon their marriage in 1854. And in it, there was a genealogical record—births, marriages, and deaths. It included a date for Frederick W. Coffin's death: 1898! Until then, my father and I had separately believed he had died around 1894. I now had a year to go on but no specific date or place of death. Still, it was information we had lacked until then. However, as it turned out, someone entered the date wrong.

Sadly, Fred Fowler Jr. passed away at age seventy-eight on February 9, 2012. Nancy, after a long illness, passed away at age seventy-five a few weeks later, on April 22, 2012. I lost a strong connection to the past once they passed away.

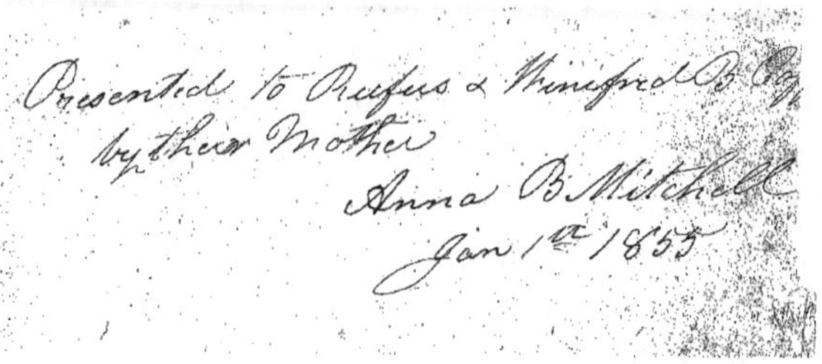

Excerpt from the Coffin family Bible (Fowler family)

A *Mayflower* Connection

Further conversations with Nancy Fowler deepened the mystery about the Coffins, including talk of a then unconfirmed *Mayflower* connection. For instance, we learned that Frederick Coffin had an exceptional lineage that could perhaps even explain part of his eagerness for adventure. One hundred two passengers were aboard the *Mayflower* in November 1620 when it arrived at what is now Plymouth, Massachusetts. There are plenty of books that document their lives and early travails. About half of these passengers died during their first winter in America. They left England and its church to worship as they thought appropriate, but because they had no legal right to settle in the new continent, they drew up the Mayflower Compact. This is the first written declaration of self-government and is often cited as a precursor of the Constitution of the United States. However, some of these voyagers were merchants interested in new settlements as a profit-making enterprise. Plymouth is the second-oldest permanent English settlement in North America, after Jamestown in Virginia.

As we researched further into Frederick Coffin's ancestry, we learned that he was descended from nine *Mayflower* passengers: Myles Standish, John Alden and Priscilla (Mullins) Alden, John Howland and Elizabeth Tilley, John and Joan (Hurst) Tilley, and William and Alice Mullins.

John Tilley, a silk worker, and his wife, Joan Hurst, both died during their first winter in Plymouth. Their orphaned daughter, Elizabeth, born around 1607, eventually married John Howland in 1624, with whom she had eleven children. The Carver family hired John Howland, who was only twenty-one when he sailed on the *Mayflower*, to assist in the migration. That he narrowly escaped death after being thrown overboard by grabbing a topsail halyard trailing in the water became a famous anecdote. The Carvers survived the winter, but both died in the spring without heirs. We descend from John Howland and Elizabeth Tilley through their daughter Desiree. John Howland held various positions in the new colony and died in 1673.

William Mullins (or Molines), with his wife, Alice, son, and daughter, Priscilla, were French Huguenots. All, except for Priscilla, died in Plymouth that first winter. Priscilla eventually married John Alden, who William Bradford had hired. Alden also held various posts in the new colony. Ironically, in later years Alden became known for his intense hatred of the Quakers and Baptists, who tried to settle on Cape Cod. He died in 1687, the last male survivor of the signers of the Mayflower Compact of 1620. Except for Mary Allerton, he was also the last survivor of the *Mayflower*'s company.

Myles Standish is perhaps the best known of our ancestral voyagers. He was born in Lancashire, England, in 1584. Unlike the other passengers, the Pilgrims hired Standish, a professional soldier, as military advisor for the Plymouth colony, but it is unclear how he connected with these voyagers. He worked on the military defense of the colony. He was also an accurate surveyor and participated in the layout of new towns. He founded Duxbury, for instance. Although he was of small stature, he had a reputation for being fierce and of quick temper. Later, he served as Plymouth's representative in England, as assistant to the governor, and as the colony's treasurer. Myles Standish is often remembered for his bravery in battle and his reputation as the military captain of the Pilgrims as well as for a character in Henry Wadsworth Longfellow's fictitious poem, "The Courtship of Myles Standish." His son Alexander married John Alden and Priscilla Mullins's daughter Sarah Alden. Standish died at an advanced age in 1656.

Year after year the Plymouth colony continued to prosper, and its inhabitants acquired new lands and established new settlements. Over time, their descendants married new settlers. Such was the case with Tristram Coffin, who founded the family line in the United States. He arrived in New England more than twenty years after the Pilgrims, in 1642. He brought with him his wife and five children, his mother, and his two unmarried sisters. He first settled in Salisbury, Massachusetts, where he lived for several years, and in 1660, he moved with his family and settled on the island of Nantucket. Unlike the *Mayflower* settlers, researchers say that he did not leave England to seek religious freedom or property and fortune. He seems to have enjoyed both, so it is unclear what motivated him to seek a new home. Ironically, he and other early settlers of Nantucket found the Puritans of Massachusetts religiously intolerant.[9]

The Coffin family first connects to the *Mayflower* descendants through the 1735 marriage of Reuben Gardner (1717–1784) to Theodate Gorham (1705–1787). Reuben was a great-grandson of Tristram Coffin, through his son

9. Louis Coffin, *The Coffin Family*.

Stephen. Theodate was the granddaughter of Desiree Howland (1623–1683) and great-granddaughter of John Howland and Elizabeth Tilley. Later on, Reuben and Theodate's granddaughter Sarah (Sally) Gardner (1762–1838) married William Coffin (1761–1850) on January 17, 1782. A second and different connection came when Betsey Parker (1800–1858) married Timothy G. Coffin (1789–1854). Betsey's mother, Averick, was a direct descendant of Myles Standish, the Aldens, and the Mullins.

Shortly after 1700, Quakerism began to take root, and by the end of the eighteenth century, the Society of Friends became the major denomination on the island, a refuge for Quakers persecuted in other areas of the Bay Colony. At the same time, Nantucket began to take off as the "Whaling Capital of the World." This lasted through the early 1800s as Nantucket became the third-largest city in Massachusetts. Nantucket was a port of call for transatlantic packets and coastal vessels and ranked third as a major port after New York and Boston.

However, the island's decline started when petroleum began to displace whale oil as an illuminant in the late 1830s. Moreover, in 1846, a brutal fire roared through Nantucket Town under the cover of night and left hundreds homeless and impoverished. About thirty-six acres were devastated, and this "Great Fire" only exacerbated the island's economic hardships. Many of its poverty-stricken inhabitants had no other alternative but to leave. Then the cry of gold from California reached Nantucket in late 1848. More than five hundred Nantucketers had sailed for the West Coast by the end of 1849, seeking new fortunes.[10]

The island was in a complete economic depression by the time of the Civil War. The population had fallen to about 6,000 in 1860, down from 9,000 in 1840. The island's population had fallen further to around 4,000 by 1870, and five years later it dropped even further, to 3,201. In the thirty years between 1840 and 1870, census figures documented the loss of 60 percent of the island's population. It is against this backdrop of the early nineteenth century that our research into the Coffin family starts.

---

10. For instance, Betsey Coffin, widow of Timothy G. Coffin, in her last will in 1858 bequeaths to her daughter-in-law Winnifred Coffin a box that her son Rufus had sent her from California. (Wait! . . . Had Rufus gone to California?)

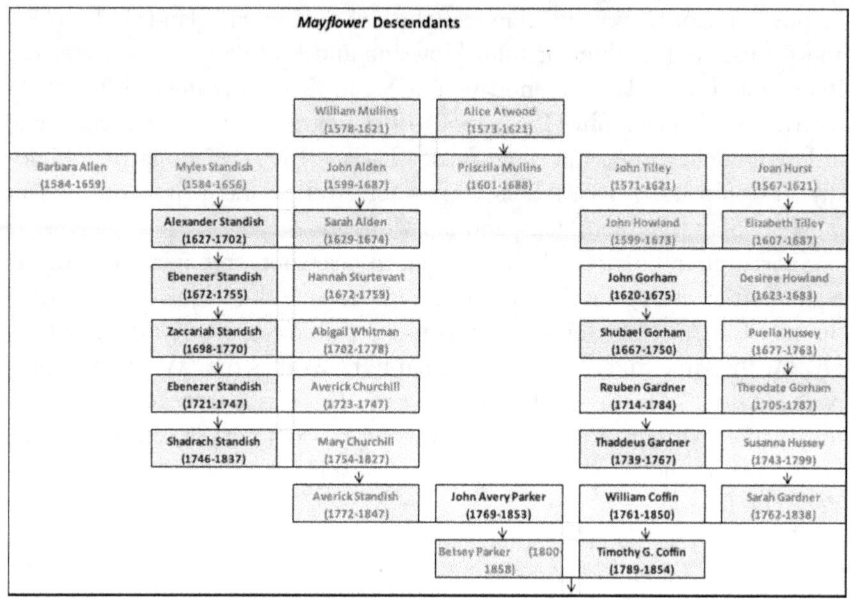

Green font = original *Mayflower* passenger
Blue background = *Mayflower* descendant
Blue font = male
Red font = female
Yellow background = no *Mayflower* ancestor

The Coffin Family in the Early 1800s

We know little of the Coffin family in the 1700s, other than basic birth, marriage, and death information. It is in the 1800s when our Coffin family gains prominence. William Coffin (1761–1850) and Sarah (Sally) Gardner's (1762–1838) son Timothy Gardner Coffin (1789–1854) married Betsey Parker (1800–1858) in April 1817, with whom he had seven children. Both of them claimed *Mayflower* ancestry. Timothy was twenty-eight and Betsey was seventeen at the time of their wedding.

William, a Quaker, was a direct descendant of Tristram Coffin through his son John. But he was also a direct descendant of *Mayflower* voyagers John Tilley and Joan Hurst, their daughter, Elizabeth, and John Howland. Betsey's mother was Averick Standish (1772–1827), a direct descendant of Myles Standish, John Alden, and the Mullins. Furthermore, Averick Standish's father, Shadrach (1746–1837), was a patriot who fought in the revolution, although he served for a limited time. Shadrach lived a long life and died at age ninety-one, very old for that era. He is buried in Plympton, Massachusetts.

Contemporary writers describe Tim as "short and thick-set, but always of impeccable dress." According to these published records, early on he engaged in a seafaring life, but upon receiving severe injuries from a fall, he turned his attention to the law.[11] He entered Brown University in Providence, Rhode Island, from which he graduated in 1813. He was admitted to the Bristol bar in 1816 as one of its earliest members. He obtained the foremost rank in the profession, "trying his intellectual strength against such opponents as Webster and Choate." He was judge advocate of Massachusetts's militia under Gen. Lincoln.

For most of his life, he resided in New Bedford, which at that time competed against Nantucket as a whaling port. New Bedford surpassed Nantucket

11. James Grant Wilson and John Fiske, eds., *Appletons' Cyclopedia of American Biography Vol. 1* (New York: D. Appleton & Co.), 677.

by 1823. According to *The History of Bristol County*,[12] he opened his law office in New Bedford and quickly became a leading attorney in the counties of Bristol, Nantucket, Dukes, Barnstable, and Plymouth. For more than forty years, he engaged in almost every case of importance in these counties before the courts. Accounts from his days indicate he was a sharp cross-examiner of his witnesses, and few witnesses could evade his keenness. He usually took the most desperate cases, typically criminal. People considered him as the most skilled lawyer in Southern Massachusetts and feared him for his violent temper.

Timothy Gardner Coffin, in an undated lithograph (signed Tim G Coffin)
Courtesy of the Nantucket Historical Association (1992.0423.001)

Following his marriage in 1817, he bought a lot at the northeast corner of Purchase and High Streets, on which he later built his house. Construction related to Route 6 replaced his dwelling with parking lots, apartment buildings, and streets on that spot. The New Bedford Directory of 1838 placed his office over 40 North Water Street. In the directory of 1839, his office is listed at 25 North Water Street and his home at 109 Purchase Street. His son Rufus's home was located at 102 Purchase Street. In 1841, Tim moved his office to 35 North Water Street, and his son Rufus was no longer listed. Both Tim and his son Rufus were freemasons.

J. Maynard, of 26 Mellen Street in Cambridge, related a famous anecdote of Tim in a short article that appeared in the local press (no date) entitled "How Judge Coffin Was Caught":

> When Judge Coffin was a young lawyer and about to plead his first case in New Bedford, not being prepared, and not wishing to acknowledge being unprepared, he arose and asked the court to excuse him, as he had been called to the sickbed of his mother. In the meantime, his mother, wishing to hear her son's first plea, had come from Nantucket and was in the gallery of the courthouse. She leaned over the

12. D. Hamilton Hurd, ed., *History of Bristol County, Massachusetts with Biographical Sketches of Many of Its Pioneers and Prominent Men* (Philadelphia: J. W. Lewis & Co., 1883).

railing, and in great indignation called down: "Timothy! Timothy! How often have I chastised thee for lying."[13]

Betsey's parents were John Avery Parker[14] (1769–1853) and Averick Standish (1772–1847). Averick was a descendant in the sixth generation from Myles Standish. John Avery Parker, born in Plympton, was New Bedford's first millionaire. He was a lineal descendant in the sixth generation from William Parker, who came from England in the 1640s and was one of the first settlers of Scituate, Massachusetts. They had at least eleven children together, including Betsey Parker Coffin. A few years after his wife's death in 1847, John married Mary Bradford Standish (1783–1868), Averick's sister and a widow.

John A. Parker made his fortune from dealings in salt, iron, and whaling. He was a shrewd and energetic businessman.[15] In 1834, he had a mansion built on County Street in New Bedford. His contemporaries considered this mansion the finest example of Greek Revival architecture in the United States, and it cost about $100,000 then (about $3.2 million today). The average house cost a fraction of that. The property was sold to developers in the early 1900s, who demolished the house and divided the land into several house lots. They only spared the south section of the mansion that still stands today.

Historical records indicate that John A. Parker was a very civic-minded individual. He founded and became the first president of the Merchants National Bank. He also served six years as state representative and three years as state senator. Although he was not well

John Avery Parker, undated photo

13. There are several sources for this anecdote. One is found in *The Friend, A Religious and Literary Journal* 38, no. 14 (1894): 298.

14. Leonard Bolles Ellis, *History of the Fire Department of the City of New Bedford, MA 1772–1890* (New Bedford, MA: E. Anthony, 1890).

15. The census of 1850 listed real estate assets valued at $134,000, or about $4.7 million today. He must have also had holdings of bonds and other securities as well as ownership interests in a multitude of businesses.

educated, he successfully brought free public schools to New Bedford (with help from his son-in-law Tim Coffin) and is responsible for today's New Bedford public school system.

Timothy G. Coffin cofounded the Merchants National Bank with his father-in-law. With his unquestioned reputation as an effective and able lawyer came a certain amount of wealth.[16] According to biographical sketches, Timothy was strong in his likes and his dislikes so that he was "a most ardent friend and a very disagreeable enemy."

Timothy and Betsey had seven children together, as described next.

RUFUS

The eldest was Rufus, born on March 29, 1819, almost one year from the day his uncle Rufus (Timothy's brother) died at sea. He is the main subject of this research. The elder Rufus, a seaman, had died in Havana, Cuba, at thirty-six years of age in 1818, unmarried, and we suspect the newborn was therefore named after him. In fact, in 1818, Timothy took the administration of the estate of his deceased brother, Rufus, as they seem to have been close. Rufus and his wife, Winnifred Chase, had numerous descendants both in the United States and in Mexico. Rufus died in Taunton, Massachusetts, in 1863 and is buried on Nantucket at Prospect Hill Cemetery. We will expand on him in the next chapter.

MARY

Mary was born on April 27, 1821. She married Rev. Thomas G. Salter (April 1, 1810–February 25, 1872), an Episcopal minister, on December 10, 1844.[17] He was born in Mansfield, Connecticut. Mary died on March 29, 1884, just shy of her sixty-third birthday, and there are references to her in family letters. Mary and her husband are buried in the family plot in New Bedford.

Mary had seven children with her husband: Mary William (1846), Jane (Jeanie) Coffin (1849–1893), Timothy Gardner Coffin (1850–1911), Thomas G. (1854), George Waldron (1856–1861), and twins Albert W. and Abby (1861). Seems the twins died the same day at only five months old that same year.

---

16. For instance, he valued his real estate at $16,400 (more than $575,000 today) in the census of 1850, which was a very large sum for the time. These figures do not include financial assets.

17. *U.S. School Yearbooks, 1880–2012* (New Haven, CT: Yale College, 1832), 239–42.

They lived in New Bedford initially but later moved to Dover, New Hampshire, where some of their children were born. The US Navy appointed Rev. Salter chaplain in 1861, and he spent four years at sea, specifically on the USS *Minnesota*. Afterward, he was stationed onshore, in Brooklyn, New York; New London, Connecticut; and Charlestown, Massachusetts, where he died suddenly in 1872. After his death, Mary received a widow's pension from the US Navy.[18] At that time the family had settled in New London, and their young daughters were recorded as having no occupation.

Once widowed, Mary moved into the household of her son-in-law Abiel Ward Nelson (1835–1913) and her daughter Jeanie, along with the other daughter, Mary W. Jeanie died in 1893 at age forty-three, with no issue. Only Mary W., Timothy, and Thomas were living in 1890. Mary W. and Thomas never married.

Timothy G. C. became a US Navy apprentice in 1866, was promoted to lieutenant in 1881, and retired in 1893, the same year he married his first wife, Rebecca, ten years younger, in Manhattan. According to the census of 1900, Thomas was single, unemployed for one year, and living with his brother Timothy and his wife in Brooklyn. After Rebecca died in 1907, Timothy married a second wife, Eva, age twenty-three, from Barbados, in 1909, according to the census of 1910. She may have been his caregiver prior to their marriage. Timothy died in 1911, at age sixty, with no mention of issue. All we learned about Thomas is that he converted to Roman Catholicism and joined the Order of the Jesuits. Their sister Jeanie disinherited her siblings in her will if any of them belonged to a Roman Catholic order. We believe there are no descendants beyond Mary's children.

JANE PARKER

Jane Parker was born on January 11, 1823, and died in 1894 at age seventy-one of a cerebral hemorrhage. She first married Gamaliel Lincoln Jr. (September 18, 1819–January 2, 1855) on December 30, 1847. He owned a clothing store. They had two children together. William Henry Lincoln was born on December 9, 1849, and we believe he died on May 12, 1880, in California. Lizzie Lincoln died at seven months of age on August 15, 1853. The young couple lived in the Timothy G. Coffin household at least initially, according to the census of 1850, with baby William. They moved soon after to 94 State

---

18. They did not report the value of their estate in the census of 1850. But they reported $4,600 (more than $150,000 in 2021) in real estate assets and $500 (about $16,500 in 2021) in personal assets in the census of 1860 and $11,000 (about $230,000 in 2021) in real estate in the census of 1870. These figures did not include the value of financial assets.

Street. Gamaliel died five years later when he was a young thirty-four years old of "rheumatism," leaving her a widow with a young son.

Jane married her second husband, George Mathewson (1816–1860), a widower, on November 2, 1858, a few weeks before her mother, Betsey, passed away. He was originally from Providence, Rhode Island, but resided in Dover, New Hampshire, at the time. Perhaps they met when Jane visited her sister Mary in Dover. George Matthewson had seven children with his first wife, Ann Maria Child (1823–1855): Sarah (1842–1912), Amey (1843–1898), Brockholst (1844–1885), Anna Maria (1847–1848), Mary (1848–1885), George (1849–1850), and Lewis (1853–1858). The census of 1860 showed the family lived in Dover. Matthewson was quite wealthy.[19] George Mathewson died six months after the census information was taken in June 1860 and only two years after he and Jane wed. He was forty-four years of age; Jane was thirty-seven.

There are no records of additional children with her second husband. Her son, William H. Lincoln, died at thirty and also left no issue. Jane never remarried, despite her youth. She is buried in the family plot in New Bedford, too, alongside her first husband, Gamaliel. Her second husband, George, is buried in Swan Point Cemetery in Providence, with his first wife.

GEORGE F.

George F. was born in 1827 and died in 1828.

WILLIAM HENRY

William was born on May 5, 1830; his parents named him after his grandfather and uncle. He married Marguerite Montgomery (1829–1900) on March 4, 1859, and died on December 15, 1884, at age fifty-four, only a few months after his older sister, Mary. His mother, Betsey, bequeathed a diamond ring and $300 to her "friend" Margaret E. Montgomery in her last will in 1858. This suggests that William and Marguerite were already in a relationship then. His marriage certificate states that he is a trader. Various censuses reported him as a farmer (1860 and 1875), with no occupation (1870), or as a laborer (1880), without a specific profession.[20]

19. He reported real estate assets of $69,000 (about $2.3 million in 2021) and personal assets of $71,000 (also about $2.3 million in 2021). These figures do not include financial assets.

20. The census of 1870 recorded real estate and personal estate totals valued each at $5,000 (a little over $100,000 in 2021).

Rufus Coffin is seated in the middle of the photograph, taken in the early 1840s. Brother William Henry Coffin is standing at the far left. Other relatives are unidentified.

He and his wife, Marguerite, settled in Providence, Rhode Island. They had two daughters who lived to adulthood: Jane Matthewson Coffin, born in 1860, and Gertrude Howland Coffin, born in 1864. A son, Timothy G. Coffin,[21] born on May 27, 1862, died when he was one year old on April 10, 1863. Their daughter Jane never married and died in 1912, at age fifty-one, in Providence. Gertrude married John Frederick Harris in 1889 and died in Boston in 1902 at age thirty-eight of heart disease, with no issue of record.

William suffered a stroke after several years of dealing with paralysis. He is buried in the family plot, with his baby son, in New Bedford. It appears that his wife, Marguerite, who died of a cerebral hemorrhage at age seventy-one in Boston in 1900, is also buried in New Bedford, but we did not find her grave. We did not find descendants beyond their two daughters.

ABBY

Abby was born in 1833 and died in 1834.

---

21. According to his tombstone in Rural Cemetery, New Bedford, he was born on May 27, 1862, and died on April 10, 1863—only a few months before his uncle Rufus died in Taunton, Massachusetts.

ABBY PARKER

Abby Parker was the youngest, born on August 9, 1835 (probably named after her sister, who died in 1834). She got engaged to her first husband, George B. Waldron (1819–1865), on September 18, 1854, one day before her father passed away. They may have wanted to get his blessing before his passing. George Waldron was originally from Stonington, Connecticut. She was only nineteen and he was thirty-five. They were married that November, one month after her older brother, Rufus, married Winnie and three months after their father died. They initially lived in New York City, where they appeared in the census of 1860.[22]

She applied for a passport in June 1862, and her husband, George, signed as a witness. We are not sure why she may have needed one. Betsey Coffin named George executor of her last will in 1858. Yet the probate had not concluded when he died in 1865 at age forty-six. Upon George's death, Abby had to share his estate with his mother, his brother (and his issue), and his executors, so she received only one-quarter of its value. He is buried in Stonington.

Not even two years later, in December 1866, Abby married her second husband, Gen. Richard Arnold (1828–1882), although we ignore how they met. He was thirty-eight years old and she was thirty-one. Richard Arnold[23] was a career US Army officer who served as a brigadier general in the Union forces during the Civil War. He enjoyed a high level of recognition in his time. They resided in Plattsburgh, New York, according to the census of 1870. They had moved to New York City by 1880, but Richard died rather suddenly only two years later on Governor's Island at age fifty-four. She never married again; she was only forty-seven years old.

She relocated to Boston, according to the census of 1890. She listed no children and bore none. She is listed as a lodger at Hotel Oxford on Huntington Avenue at that time. She died of "hemiplegia traumatic" on October 2, 1904, aged sixty-nine, the last of the siblings to pass away. She had suffered an unspecified accident in September 1900 that left her half-paralyzed. Most of her wealth was used for her medical care. She appears to be quite bitter in her

---

22. In 1860, George Waldron listed his real estate assets at $10,000 (about $330,000 today) and personal assets also at $10,000, while she listed real estate assets at $5,000 (about $160,000) and personal assets at $20,000 (about $660,000).

23. Richard Arnold was the son of Rhode Island governor and US congressman Lemuel Arnold. He was born in Providence, Rhode Island, in 1828 and graduated from the US Military Academy in 1850. Arnold was promoted to captain in the Regular Army and became an aide-de-camp to Maj. Gen. John E. Wool. Arnold commanded Battery D of the Second US Artillery at the First Battle of Bull Run. His sister Sally was married to Union Brig. Gen. Isaac P. Rodman, who was mortally wounded at the Battle of Antietam.

will, dated 1902. She included only her nieces Gertrude[24] and Jane M. Coffin, among others, but explicitly excluded her nephew Rufus Coffin or any living Salter relatives, stating that "they had forfeited by neglect all claims upon me, or upon any estate I may die possessed of." Most of the legatees were a few cousins on her mother's side and relatives from her husband's side. She asked to be buried with her second husband, Richard Arnold, at Swan Point Cemetery in Providence, Rhode Island, her epitaph to read, "He giveth his beloved sleep."

Timothy G. Coffin died on September 19, 1854, only a few weeks before his children Rufus and Abby married in November and just shy of his sixty-fifth birthday, after a long, continued, yet undefined illness. He signed his lengthy last will on June 28, 1854, in which he disposed of some of his most

24. Gertrude Coffin Harris died only a couple of weeks after the will's signing and was dead when Abby died in 1904.

valued personal possessions.[25] In its obituary notice two days later, the *Mercury* stated, "We are pained to announce his death" and went on to note that "he will be missed in our courts, and he will not be less missed in a community of which he was an ornament." The *Standard*'s tribute was: "In private life, he was distinguished for his congenial and urbane disposition, his kindness of heart, and his unostentatious generosity. He was a firm friend, a kind parent, and an indulgent husband."

His body lies in Rural Cemetery in New Bedford, where his children erected a monument in his memory (above). His wife, Betsey, died four years later in 1858 of stomach cancer and is buried next to him. She left an estate valued at $92,252.08 (a little over $3 million in 2021) that was settled in probate court in 1869, eleven years after her death. Other family members are also buried in the same plot: their daughter Mary C. Salter and her husband, Rev. Thomas Salter; their son William H. Coffin and his baby son, Timothy G. Coffin; and their daughter Jane C. Mathewson with her first husband, Gamaliel Lincoln, and their baby daughter Lizzie. Actually, from the dates on the gravestones, it seems that Lizzie was the first one to be buried at the family plot. We suspect that Mary's son, George W., and her twins, Abby and Albert, may be buried in Dover, New Hampshire, where they lived at the time of their deaths.

Family members not buried in the family plot include William's wife, Marguerite (who died in Boston); Jane's second husband, George Mathewson (buried in Providence); Tim and Betsey's eldest son, Rufus (who is buried at Prospect Hill Cemetery on Nantucket); and Abby Parker and her second husband, Richard Arnold, both of whom are buried in Swan Point Cemetery in Providence.

A few months before the passing of Timothy G. Coffin, his father-in-law, John A. Parker, died at the age of eighty-four on December 30, 1853. The official death record states "general debility and influenza," but historical records suggest that he may have been poisoned. Contemporary accounts affirmed that he sent his servant to the basement of his house for a bottle of cider. Shortly after that, he became ill and died. Averick Standish, who preceded him in death, is buried in the family plot. We understand his estate took more than twenty years to settle in probate court because of its complexity. Their monument can be seen third in the background in the photo on the previous page, also in Rural Cemetery in New Bedford.

---

25. He bequeathed his law library to the people of the Island of Nantucket. He also left $100 to each of his sons-in-law for them to purchase an item to remember him for, stating that "I am most happy to say, of both of them, that all their conduct toward me has been respectful, attentive and affectionate since they have been members of my family."

John Avery, Timothy, and Betsey died as the United States more than doubled in size and had captured lands that extended west to the Pacific. These families had enjoyed wealth and a high social standing for about fifty years. But slowly the fortunes of this family eroded, and their children and grandchildren were unable to achieve the same. These families and their immediate descendants would be mostly gone by the end of the century.

Incidentally, at about the same time in 1853, new families emerged south of the border, which would be key in perpetuating their memory. In a small, dusty town in Northern Mexico, a young couple was forming a new family. In due course, one of their daughters would marry one of Timothy's grandsons when he traveled to that country and would provide a significant link between both countries. Despite whatever disappointments we may speculate Rufus gave his parents, it would be only through him that Timothy G. Coffin would have numerous descendants in both countries well into the new millennium.

Rufus Coffin and His Family

Timothy G. Coffin must have been a tough act to follow. Rufus might not have been as focused or successful in the ways his father wanted him to be. Moreover, from published records, we glean that Timothy was of high morals and standards. So was the Parker family and those who married into it. In fact, given what we know about Timothy, possibly Rufus might not have lived up to his father's high expectations. The Catalogue of the Officers and Students of Brown University for the academic year 1836–1837 showed him as part of the sophomore class, with residence in New Bedford. However, the college dismissed him in 1837, and he never graduated. We ignore the circumstances. His parents surely must have been displeased.

To the eyes of someone living in the twenty-first century, Rufus might have suffered from learning disabilities, nearly impossible to diagnose back then. Or perhaps it was then that he took to excessive drinking. We are certain that he did not obtain a college degree, as his father must have wanted him to. Both his grandfather John and his father, Tim, enjoyed great success. Therefore, his parents might not have been pleased with Rufus, unable to join his father's successful law practice.[26] We could also speculate that he grew up in an environment of wealth, which perhaps inhibited his drive for financial success. This may have given Rufus a false sense of comfort and security and perhaps contributed to problematic family relations as well. For instance, his mother chose her son-in-law George Waldron as executor of her will and not her own sons, Rufus or William.

In any event, we do not know how Rufus earned his living. The census of 1850 in New Bedford did not specify a profession for him, even though he was thirty years old. That census also showed him living in his father's household, alongside his sister Jane and her husband, Gamaliel, and the other unmarried siblings. But we know little of his life before his marriage. Ten years later, his parents

26. Timothy bequeathed his prized law library to the people of Nantucket through the Coffin School.

were deceased, and he became the head of a household. The census of 1860 recorded his profession as a merchant marine,[27] with residence in Nantucket. Recall that his grandfather John A. Parker was in the business of building vessels, and maybe this provided Rufus with an incentive to become one.

Rev. Ethan Allen married Rufus and Winnifred (Winnie) Bunker Chase on Nantucket on November 1, 1854, at the then newly built St. Paul's Episcopal Church on 20 Fair Street. They were both thirty-five years of age, which, for a woman at the time, was quite old. His father, Timothy, had just passed away in September, and not even a year earlier, his wealthy grandfather John A. Parker had passed away too. He might have benefited financially from his father's and grandfather's estates, although this would have taken some time to settle in those days.

Winnifred B. Coffin in an undated photograph
W. Kuntz portrait, courtesy of the Nantucket Historical Association (P260)

We believe Rufus met Winnie when he traveled to Nantucket as a merchant marine. There could have been a connection also with her stepfather, Frederick Mitchell, who was a wealthy merchant. We ignore, however, how long their courtship lasted. After his father's death, Rufus settled in Nantucket with his new wife and appears to have been close to her small family, in sharp contrast to the numerous cousins he had from both his father's and his mother's sides.

Winnie's parents were Daniel Coffin Chase (1792–1834) and Anna Bunker (1797–1875). Daniel's parents were Peter Chase (1764–1842) and Elizabeth Hussey (1766–1847). His grandmother was Anna Coffin, married to Batchelder Hussey. Daniel was one of ten children, and he died suddenly when he was forty-two years old in New York City. He was also buried in Manhattan. Winnie was only fifteen years old then. Anna had first married Daniel in late

27. A merchant marine was a sailor or captain working for a commercial vessel or ship.

Annie Bunker Mitchell in an undated photograph
E. T. Kelley portrait, courtesy of the Nantucket Historical Association (CDV1361)

1818. Winnie was born within the following year. There is no record of other sibling—certainly none living to adulthood.

Anna was one of three daughters born to Latham Bunker (1755–1827) and Susannah Barnard (1761–1836): Lydia, the eldest, died unmarried at the age of thirty in 1824. Anna was the middle daughter, born in 1797. The youngest, Sarah, died at age eighty-two in 1882. She was the second wife of Josiah Coleman (1794–1870) and had no children, even though she was still quite young when she married. There are references to Sarah in correspondence between Rufus and his mother-in-law and stepfather-in-law.

Anna, widowed at a relatively young age and with no parents, married Frederick W. Mitchell (1784–1867) in 1845 when she was forty-eight years old and he was sixty, ten years after her husband, Daniel, died. She may have needed financial stability. It was the second marriage for both of them. Frederick W. Mitchell had been first married to Eunice Russell (1786–1843), with whom he had no children of his own. Since Winnie's grandparents Peter and Elizabeth Chase died in the 1840s, we do not know whether Winnie was able to maintain a strong relationship with them or her uncles and aunts despite her father's death. Some of them lived well into their eighties and nineties.

For the next nine years, until her marriage to Rufus in 1854, Winnie lived with her stepfather and mother, and it appears that she remained close to them until their deaths. The census of 1860 showed the young Coffin family living next door to the Mitchells. Since Frederick W. Mitchell had no children, Rufus and Winnie named their first son after Winnie's stepfather. That is why he carried a drawing of his likeness with him to Mexico, the closest to a grandfather figure for him.[28]

28. His grandmother Betsey did have a brother, Frederick Parker (1806–1861).

Winnie's mother, Anna Bunker Mitchell, presented Rufus and Winnie with a family Bible on January 1, 1855. The Fowler family owns this Bible. It holds important facts about the Timothy Coffin genealogical record, as we showed earlier.

Rufus and Winnie had four children during their short marriage:

1. Frederick William, my great-grandfather, was born on August 28, 1855, ten months after their wedding. Although it may seem strange that Rufus would not name his son after himself or his father, we note that his sister Mary already had named her first son Timothy Gardner Coffin Salter, born in 1849. But it does seem odd nonetheless that he would name his firstborn after his wife's stepfather. He died in Mexico, leaving behind two young daughters.
2. Rufus Jr. was born on November 12, 1857. He married Amy Ingraham in 1910, and he died in Boston in 1924, at age sixty-seven. He also left behind two young daughters.
3. Anna (Annie) Mitchell was born on May 26, 1859. Her parents named her after Winnie's mother. Annie died when she was thirteen years old on July 13, 1872. The *Nantucket Inquirer* reported her death on July 14, 1872. The cause of death is recorded as "apoplexy," but that can be a confusing term. She is buried at Prospect Hill Cemetery on Nantucket with her parents. We saw her picture earlier.
4. Betsey (Bessie) Parker, named after Rufus's mother, was born on April 10, 1861—before Rufus's first commission with the US Revenue Service. She died on March 12, 1865, of scarlet fever and is also buried at Prospect Hill Cemetery on Nantucket.

At least for a short while after Frederick was born, the young family lived in New York City, although records show that Rufus Jr. was born in New Bedford. But the family's happiness did not last. Long periods of separation resulted at first from Rufus's commercial maritime activities and later from war assignments. Illness began almost at the same time as the war and resulted in premature death. Then both girls died young soon after their father died in 1863. It must have been devastating for Winnie to lose both daughters, especially after first losing her husband. Overall, however, it seems that theirs was initially a happy marriage.

Several letters attest to a very affectionate relationship. Here is one example, in a letter from New York City, addressed to Winnie's mother, Anna B. Mitchell:

Washington Hotel
New York, Feb 19 1856

My dear Mother,

Winnie received yesterday two letters from home—one from yourself and one from Father—for which she sends you many thanks.

She has had many an uneasy and troubled moment in your account for the reason that the ice has so completely hemmed you in, and made communication less accessible to you than though you were on the other side of the Atlantic. This has indeed been a severe winter not only to you, but throughout the land. Such cold weather was never before known in this city that is such a long successive term. The jingling of sleigh bells is still heard in the streets and in most streets a sleigh runs easier than a carriage—Broadway however is in a doleful plight and though hundreds of laborers are employed to endeavor to make it passable the stages are still far above the sidewalks and it will be some time before the pavement is clear. Many of the streets are entirely impracticable for use, and must remain so till the Sun sends many more genial days than he has lately favored us with to liquidize the compact mass of ice with which they are covered.

We too have been ice bound and we continue so—for since you have been shut out from the world the "Ice King" has blockaded Long Island Sound in such a way that no vessel can pass. No steamer has passed in the time to Stonington, Hartford or Fall River or any of the Sound Harbors and I am told that the ice at Throgs Pt. is still three feet in the kniss rock with every prospect of it continuing so—None can tell how long. Our city rail roads have been only lately freed from the same obstruction and in Brooklyn no cars can run. In fact, all are here satisfied that we have had snow and ice enough for one winter and a sight of mother earth will be hailed with a general rejoicing from one and all. You cannot possibly imagine what a plight our streets are in—Broadway especially—Horses cannot now get along faster than a walk and the stages go oftener empty than full for the reason that one finds it more comfortable to walk than to be jolted nearly to death in a stage. There are often seen stages, carts, etc. stuck fast in holes that the horses by their best endeavors cannot extricate them from except by unloading and extra assistance. The weather continues very cold as may be seen by referring to Prof. Merriam's diary published daily in the New York Herald, and we have no reason to expect better things for some time to come.

Notwithstanding all this I am happy to inform you that Winnie and the prodigy enjoy their usual good health, and that both appear happy and contented. Winnie likes her quarters here and considers herself very pleasantly situated. We have a parlor and bedroom on the same floor with the room Jem occupied when here. And they are good and warm rooms. Winnie can here get enough to eat, and could you see her make way with the good things of the table you would have no cause to complain of her appetite unless you had serious thoughts of inviting her to spend some time with you at home. Freddy seems to like the arrangement entirely for we have a good nurse who takes them all about the house and he is frequently invited into the ladies room and receives from them much notice and attention. The ladies parlor is his play room, and from the windows facing on Broadway he sees all that is going on there. He does not walk yet though we expect that it will not be long before we shall have to notify you that he does and that his legs have caused his head to receive many a contusion. We shall have soon to provide something different than lacteal food for him for he has provided himself with a couple of teeth and there is every prospect of his getting more. His mother says he bites. At any rate she makes awful faces sometimes & cries out most lustily.

Winnie receives no calls now. Occasionally someone drops in to see Freddy, and he does all in his power to entertain them. His nurse says that the ladies of the house call him Captain Coffin for they say he is the Captain of all babies in the house. But I hardly think it worthwhile to say much more about him for when you can inform us that the boats can make a landing of their passengers at the wharf instead of at the place not found in any of "her British Majesty's Charts" we shall try to bring him to you and permit you to have ocular demonstrations of his abilities. In the meantime, we hope to hear often from you, and that you continue well. And we may add have some little consideration for horse flesh for by all account old general will gladly rejoice when the melting of the snow will permit him to cease from his labors, and be for a time at rest. And now dear Mother, with much love from your daughter and myself to you and Father believe me

Your very affect[ionate] Son
R. Coffin

As a merchant marine, Rufus had to travel great distances and was absent for long stretches at a time.[29] I was able to obtain a photocopy of one of his letters to Frederick ("Freddy"):

Ship Charles Cooper[30]
At sea July 30, 1859
Lat 40.37 Long. 2°31 East

My dear boy Freddy,

Your papa expects to be very soon near Marseilles, and for fear that he may had not have time then, he sits himself down now to write his little boy a long letter. Your papa has no one to speak to all the way from Antwerp, has had no one to sit at the table with him, and he has been quite lonesome. He has thought very often how he wished he had his little boy with him, and what good times we would have had. Freddy's pig, just before we got to Antwerp had eight of the prettiest

29. Betsey Coffin in her last will and testament written in 1858 bequeathed Winnie a box that Rufus sent her from California, so we think he had been a merchant marine for some time.

30. The *Charles Cooper* was built in Black Rock, Connecticut, in 1856. It is the best surviving wooden square-rigged American merchant ship meant for packet trade. It began with regular fixed schedules between New York and Antwerp. Carolus Ludovi-cus Weyts (Belgian, 1828–1875) painted the ship: "Ship Charles Cooper of New York, Capt. R. Coffin Passing Flushing," 1858.

little piggies you ever saw and they were all white, but one—and he had each little black spots all over him about as large as a ten cent piece and he is a beauty. Now when the old pig got the little ones it was in the night and blowing a gale and when we found them in the morning, four of them were dead, and the others we had to wrap up in cotton, and put them in the galley besides the cook's stove, or they would have died too. Well soon after when the weather got warm the little things would run about decks as lively as so many little kittens, but after we had been a week in Antwerp, the mother died, and papa had to send the little ones into the country, and have them fed on milk till they got large enough to take care of themselves onboard ship. Papa wishes his little boy was here to see them now. They have grown so large & plump.

Papa has also a little dog, just two months old that was given [to] him in Antwerp. He is about half as large as Aunt Abby's "Fan"—He is as white as a snow drop. Not a black mark about him—has a little short tail, and cropped ears, and his hair sticks up all over him, just like pig's bristles, he is the homeliest looking dog you ever saw but he is very good, and when he gets larger, he will catch all the rats that eat up papa's clothes. He and the pigs have great times together, especially after dinner when we give the dog the chicken bones for then the pigs come, and try to steal his dinner, and then he barks and bites the pigs' ears. And they bite him, and papa has to have one of the boys to stand by to whip away the pigs, so that the little dog can eat her dinner. Now if my little Freddy were here, he would not let the pigs eat up the little dog's dinner. Would you Freddy? Her name is Josephine, but I call her "Phine." Now when the ship gets back to New York, papa wants you to come on, and see him, and he will show you the dog, and he thinks you will like him very much.

Now what does my little boy think his papa has found on board [this] ship belonging to him? Why he found in the pantry his large Picture Book with the Zoological gardens and Puss in Boots, and he has found the book that had the story of "What a Sad Catastrophe?" and "The Horses Knew Both Beans & Corn," and he has found Freddy's ball, and has them all put away in the table drawer, where Freddy used to sit up to work on his altitude [?].

When papa gets in port he is going to look all around the shops to see if he can find a Water Card, and if he don't [*sic*] he will find something else that he knows will please his little boy, and something for bubby Rufus and the baby. You must tell Mother that she must pack the baby up in a box, and send her out here, so that papa can see her, and he will send her right back by telegraph. That would be a funny way, don't you think so Freddy boy?

Now papa wants his little boy to behave very well. And as soon as he is old enough, Mother will send him to school, where he can learn to read, and write, and then he can sit down, and write his papa a long letter, and tell him all about affairs at home—about grandmamma, grandpapa, and Mother, bubby & the baby, and about the hens and chickens and how many eggs he gets every day, and about going to Aunt Sarah's, and getting gingerbread from her closet and all such things. And then papa will bring him home a splendid writing desk, so that he can have a place for his pens and pencils and paper, with a lock and key to it. And he shall have a gold watch to wear in his pocket so as to tell when it is time to go to School, without having to ask anyone to tell him what time it is. And then he shall go to Antwerp in the ship with papa and see Mrs. Bailey's little girls, who want to see him very much and send a great deal of love to him, and No. 69, wanted to know why I did not bring him this time, and I told him, that Freddy was staying home to help Mama to take care of his little brother.

Well Freddy, don't you think your papa has written you a long letter? You must tell grandpapa all about it, and tell him that your papa thanks him very much for cementing the cellar to your house, and ask him, in the yard, if he thinks there is room enough to build a little stable for your pony when you get one, because when that baby gets big enough Freddy must take her out to drive. And now good bye, my dear boy, till I get time to write you again. Kiss Mama, bubber Rufus and the baby, and tell them papa sent them each a kiss all the way from Marseilles.

Your affect[ionate] Father
Rufus Coffin

From these letters and census records, it appears that Winnie Chase was very close to her mother, Annie, and her stepfather, Frederick W. Mitchell.

The first military records we find of Rufus are from August 21, 1861, when he received the commission of first lieutenant,[31] shortly after the birth of their daughter Bessie. President Abraham Lincoln signed his appointment, effective August 8, 1861 (see below).[32]

Despite his experience, he failed to obtain a captaincy because he did not know gunnery.[33] The collector at New York ordered he head to Baltimore, and he was assigned the command of the *Hercules* that same month, a commendable achievement. The *Hercules* was one of three steam tugboats purchased from the Patapsco Steam Tug Company of Baltimore for $9,000 each.

The other tugboats were *Reliance* and *Tiger*. Revenue Capt. John McGowan took possession of the steamboat on August 10, 1861, and it was fitted under his supervision. The collector at New York commissioned the *Hercules* on

31. Records of Officers, US Revenue Marine.

32. He was commissioned first lieutenant in the Revenue Marine Service, which belonged to the Department of the Treasury and not the US Navy. That is why the government rejected Winnie's request for a pension after the war, because there was no law allowing benefits to a widow of a Revenue Cutter officer.

33. Florence Kern, *The United States Revenue Cutters in the Civil War* (Bethesda, MD: Alised Enterprises, 1988).

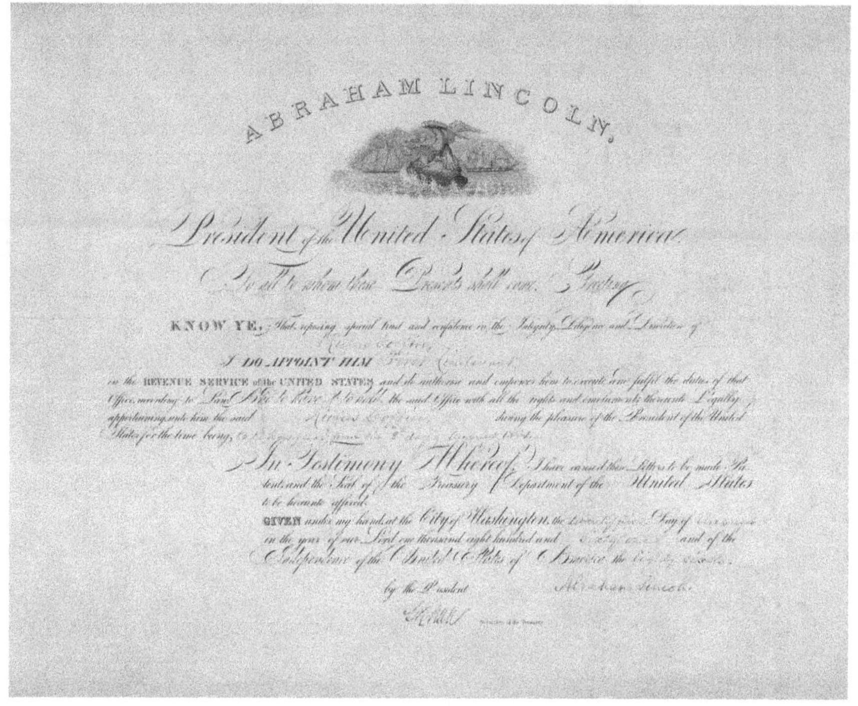

September 11, 1861, under Rufus's command. She was placed under orders of Gen. John A. Dix at Fort McHenry and operated on the Rappahannock River and the Chesapeake Bay. There are numerous citations of Rufus Coffin in Gen. Dix's correspondence when Rufus cruised in Pocomoke Bay and Tangier's Sound. Sadly, by December 1861, his superiors suspended Rufus amid charges of intoxication.[34]

We here reproduce a transcript of a letter from this time to his father-in-law:

U.S. Gun Boat Hercules
Balt. 13 Oct [18]61

My dear Father,

I have just returned from another cruise down the Chesapeake Tangier & Pocomoke Sounds and up the Potomac. I have overhauled, and examined a large number of vessels and have been very busy.

For several days we have had very severe weather, heavy gales from N and S. NE then and have had to seek harbor for anchorage according to the direction of the wind. The presence of our three-gun boats in these waters has nearly broken up the illegal traffic that lately was

---

34. We wonder if doctors missed a more definitive illness and confused the symptoms with intoxication given the limited medical knowledge at that time.

Rufus Coffin, ca. 1861–1862

so largely carried on in these waters though I am quite certain that some of it is still carried on very secretly.

On Smith & Tangier Islands I am glad to say there is not a single Secesher. All are for the Union and such is fast getting to be the code in the lower Counties of Maryland. There are many however who have long carried on a trade with the Virginians living as they do just on the boundary line, who think it hard their trade should be stopped but I have said to them that every dollar they pay for Virginia Potatoes goes so far toward prolonging the war and helping the enemy, and they quietly acquiesce to this view. What has transpired in the world since my leaving Balt. I am as ignorant of as possible. I have not seen a paper for a long time & consequently have no news of any importance to give you except about myself and my doings while cruising in the Pocomoke.

I was unfortunate enough to lose my canoe—she was swamped in a heavy sea and before we could haul her up alongside she filled and we had to cut her line and let her go. She was a beauty 30 ft long schooner rigged and sailed like the wind. She was worth $80. This is the craft I took on my first cruise with a man in her on his way to Virginia. He was released by Maj. Gen. Dix on taking the oath of allegiance but his vessel was condemned as a prize. I had found her very useful in sending an armed crew on shore as she sailed very fast, and would carry a dozen men easily and we could land in her more easily than in a boat.

I have written to Freddy and shall expect you will read his letters to him as he is scarcely able yet to do it himself and I hope you will encourage him to make all due progress in his studies so that he will soon be able to write his papa and to read his answers. I shall write to Winnie soon and she must consider this the same as though directed to her. Give her my best love. And tell her to kiss all the children Freddie, Rufus, Annie and Bessie, and with my love & best wishes to yourself & mother.

I remain affect[ionately] your Son

R. Coffin

As it turned out, in early 1862, his superiors reprimanded Rufus and detached him from the *Hercules*. Rufus next took command of the *Jackson* in Baltimore later on but almost immediately was transferred to the *Tiger* in New York. He was moved from the *Tiger* to the *Flora* in March 1862, and he sailed to Port Royal, South Carolina. There were charges brought against him for seemingly delaying its departure to that port and that he was remiss in duty. He was ultimately acquitted and praised for his navigating skills. In May 1862, they told him to report to command the *Morris* at Boston and then the *Toucey* a few months later. In August, the *Toucey* was ordered to Castine, Maine, and she remained there throughout the war.

We have a copy of an undated letter he wrote his father-in-law from the *Jackson*:

My dear Father,

I wrote Winnifred on Sunday evening notifying her of my arrival here. On Monday I reported myself on board this cutter and took charge as executive officer. Capt. Cornell who by the way is a very excellent gentleman, and a perfect officer and who married a Nantucket woman Harriet C. Earle, which is certainly proof of that face (do you know her?) If so please inform me, says that he thinks he shall shortly be ordered somewhere else, and then I will be put in command of this cutter. I of course asked him no questions, only saying that I should be pleased to have such a command. It being winter time the crew has been reduced to 30 men, which is more than sufficient, although by no means her compliment. We have to board all vessels that go out examine vessel and papers and it keeps the officers & crew here busy from sunrise till sunset, at which time we strike our colors and allow no vessels to leave the harbor. Today we boarded 35 outward bound, and 40 came into port. I have three officers beside myself, 2d & 3d lieutenant and pilot who acts as boarding officer. In December as many as 130 vessels were boarded in a single day going out (we do not board those coming in) and as many as 2300 during the month. You can by this statement form some idea of the commerce in this city.

I am much pleased with this cutter. My accommodations are much preferable to those of the Hercules. And I am particularly pleased with my messmates.

The Captain has his private quarters and messes by himself. We have our separate room and mess by ourselves taking our meals at precisely the same hours that you do except the breakfast, which you know is always served at 8 oc (sic) on ship board. It has now struck 7 bells and the boatswain has piped down hammocks. And here sit three officers in the ward room all busily engaged in letter writing. Mr. Dickinson, the pilot writing to his wife. Mr. Holloway to his sweetheart, and I to you, and when we have all done we may engage in a friendly chat for an hour and then to bed, before you get through your game of whist. We don't play cards here. All such games being strictly prohibited.

Today I have been the officer in command and tomorrow I shall be off duty, and shall probably be on shore most of the day, and in the evening I am invited to go to the theatre to hear and see that charming little actress Miss Maggie Mitchell.[35] Winnie went with me to see her in Boston & we took Freddie with us. Ask them please if they remember her.

We burn kerosene oil here in just such a lamp as we had at the house the evening before I left, and it gives a brilliant light. I saw on board the Steamer Bay State a very different burner which increases the light one half. In turning the elevating screw you do not turn up the wick but the shield that covers it and thus have a great light or a small one at pleasure. The wick is trimmed hollowing in the center and thus more light is given.

Please say to Winnie that I safely delivered the package entrusted to my care for Mrs. Parkhurst. It is past 8 bells the watch is called, and we are all snug for the night. I shall light a cigar and when done inhaling its perfume shall retire till all hands are piped to breakfast and so good night to you and all at home and with my best love to you and them.

I remain your affect[ionate] Son

R. Coffin

Still, the *Nantucket Inquirer* reported on June 17, 1862, that Rufus had come back to the island for a short visit to his family and recovery of his health. He was recovering from typhoid fever.

35. Maggie Mitchell (1832–1918). According to Wikipedia, the petite, always youthful comedienne began her stage career with walk-on roles while still a child. At the age of twenty-one, she had an extended engagement in Cleveland that precipitated a "Maggie Mitchell craze" in that city and led to her first starring tour of the regional theaters. Mitchell did not achieve national celebrity, however, until 1861, when she appeared in the title role of *Fanchon, the Cricket*—a light, sentimental comedy adapted from a story by George Sand. Her sprightly performance captivated audiences and critics alike and brought her overnight stardom. Mitchell continued playing the role of Fanchon for the next twenty-five years and counted Abraham Lincoln, Ralph Waldo Emerson, and Henry Wadsworth Longfellow among her many admirers.

Captain Rufus Coffin.—Captain Rufus Coffin, of the United States
Revenue Service has been here on a short visit to his family, and for
the recovery of his health. He was quite sick in New York for several
weeks, with the typhoid fever, after his return from Port Royal. Since
being in this service, he has had command of the US Revenue steamer
Hercules, on the Chesapeake, for a short time was Executive officer of
the US Revenue Cutter *Jackson,* at Baltimore, and was then ordered
to the command of the US steamer *Tiger,* stationed at the Narrows
at New York, from which steamer he was ordered to the US Revenue
steamer *Flora,* to go out to Port Royal. On his way out, he stopped at
Fortress Monroe, for coal—and left the morning of the day that the
conflict took place between the *Monitor* and the *Merrimac.* On his way
to Port Royal, when off Charleston, in the night at 2 am., he was fired
at four times by the *Augusta,* one the blockading squadron. Captain C.
had all his lights hoisted, and was running his course down the Coast.
When the firing commenced, he did not stop, but run to the nearest
ship, the "*Flambeau,*" stopped his steamer, and asked the meaning of
his being fired at, and was told that they thought he was a rebel trying to run into Charleston. He was soon boarded by Mr. Watson, an
officer from the *Augusta,* and proper explanations having passed, proceeded on his way. The fleet was laying far out in deep water, and it
was very singular that they should suspect any vessel would attempt to
run the blockade in so conspicuous manner. No vessel had been seen
on board the steamer till two shots had been fired and signal lights
were hoisted throughout the fleet. The Quartermaster's transport
(steamer *Oriental*) was also fired at by the same ship, while on her way
to Port Royal, a few days after the affair with the *Flora.* Captain C. now
leaves us to go to Boston, to take command of the US Revenue cutter
Morris, and we are told that he has received very flattering testimoni-
als from the Secretary of the Treasury for the very skillful manner in
which he managed the affairs of the *Flora.* We wish him success in his
new craft, and we feel no one will strike a heavier blow in our country's
cause than he, when an opportunity presents.—[*Nantucket Inquirer*]

Official reports of illness resurfaced in October 1862 in Castine, Maine,
and Rufus left his commission in November on account of his illness. He
signed his last will on January 23, 1863, probably because the wills of his
grandfather John A. Parker and his parents were still in probate court, and it
was better protection for his family. He was so ill that he could sign his signa-
ture only with an *X.* On July 13, 1863, the navy revoked his commission and
dismissed him for insanity (officially, it was "delirium tremens," or a severe
form of alcohol withdrawal). He then departed Castine. Official records point
to excessive drinking as the cause for his illness and that "he would have been
dismissed a year earlier had it not been for his illness." The reality is that it
was easier to blame his physical condition on intoxication than on a physical
illness or the lingering effects of typhoid fever. We will never know.

Gravesite of Rufus Coffin and Winnifred Bunker Coffin—Nantucket, Prospect Hill Cemetery

He died not too long afterward at the Hospital for the Insane in Taunton, Massachusetts, on August 9, 1863, at forty-four years of age—the official military record states insanity, but his death certificate in Nantucket mentions paralysis. Without a proper autopsy, it is unclear what his true ailment was. Winnie's pension application to the US Congress in 1881 states that he had "contracted Southern fever at Port Royal, S.C., which produced paralysis of the brain from which he died." Legislators rejected the application the following month on the basis that there is "no law allowing the widow of a Revenue Cutter officer pension." One more blow to deal with. We believe he was in transit from Castine to Nantucket via New Bedford, intending to get back to the island to convalesce, or perhaps he had been told that he had not much longer to live.

Whatever the situation, instead of laying his body to rest with those of his parents in New Bedford, which is very close to Taunton, Winnie had Rufus's body transferred to Nantucket for burial at Prospect Hill Cemetery. Perhaps keeping his body nearby provided needed comfort. What had begun as a happy marriage ended sadly in a premature death. The sudden death of their young daughters soon after compounded Winnie's grief.

Once widowed, Winnie moved in with her mother and stepfather at 69 Main Street.[36] Although her main source of income was gone, she may

36. The Frederick Mitchell house, built in 1834, a brick structure, at 69 Main Street. Two men in top hats and two women are posed on the front steps. Note the two other women looking out of windows on the right side of the house. Verso reads: 69 Main St., Church Haven.

Frederick W. Mitchell house, 69 Main Street, Nantucket
Courtesy of the Nantucket Historical Association (P2266)

have benefitted from disbursements from the estates of Timothy and Betsey Coffin. By 1870, Frederick W. Mitchell had passed away too. Frederick Mitchell was extremely well-to-do by those days' standards.[37]

Although his early years might have been happy ones, young Frederick experienced personal loss and tragedy from a very young age. First, his father in 1863—he must have had only vague memories of him when he grew up. Two years later his younger sister, Bessie, died of scarlet fever. He must have grown close to the only grandfather (not by blood) he knew, Frederick W. Mitchell, who died when Frederick was twelve years old in December 1867 from "cancer and abscess." When he was sixteen, his other sister, Annie (1872),[38] suddenly passed away from apoplexy, which at the time referred to

37. The census of 1850 listed the value of his real estate at $8,000 (about $280,000 in 2021). In 1860, he valued his real estate at $6,000 (almost $200,000 in 2021) and his personal estate at $31,000 (more than $1 million in 2021). In contrast, Rufus valued his real estate at $2,000 ($65,000 in 2021) and his personal estate at $3,000 ($100,000 in 2021). In 1870, Anna Mitchell was widowed, and she valued her real estate at $5,000 ($100,000 in 2021) and her personal estate at $7,000 ($145,000 in 2021); Winnie, living with her, had real estate of $1,200 ($25,000 in 2021) and a personal estate of $200 (4,000 in 2021), and children Frederick and Rufus Jr. listed personal estates of $50 ($1,000 in 2021) each, probably what their grandmother Betsey Parker bequeathed to them.

38. Frederick must have been close to his sister and grandmother, both named Annie, since he named his firstborn daughter Anita, and after her premature death, he named his third daughter Ana.

the sudden loss of consciousness related perhaps to an aneurism. Three years later, in 1875, his beloved grandmother Anna passed away, too, from "paralysis" a few days short of her seventy-eighth birthday.

The census of 1870 listed Frederick Coffin's profession as "seaman," perhaps following in his father's footsteps, which implies he worked for a wage and was not a student, despite his young age. In 1871, his cousin William H. Lincoln, age twenty-one, registered to vote in San Francisco, and California may have been beckoning.[39] Moreover, going to college like his grandfather or father may not have been an option or even a desire. Winnie benefitted from Frederick Mitchell's estate when her mother, Anna, died. Deed records show that Winnie inherited the Mitchell house upon her mother's death in 1875. Five years later Winnie turned it over legally to Rufus Jr. despite the fact she still lived in it and was renting out rooms to summer visitors. While it seems strange that Winnie overlooked Frederick, this and the fact that he does not show up in other rosters after 1879 suggest he had left the island already. The census of 1880 did not pick up Frederick Coffin's name anymore in the United States. We are not certain he attended the first Coffin family reunion held on the island in 1881 either.

There was not much to hold him in Nantucket—of his closest family, only his mother and younger brother survived; his father's siblings also were alive, but perhaps they were not close. The 1880 census, however, placed Rufus Jr., twenty-three years old, living in a boarding house in Boston, working as a clerk for a bank. Winnie lived alone on Main Street in Nantucket, renting rooms to summer visitors, likely seeking additional income. However, Winnie appears to have lived, at least part-time, with Rufus in Brookline during the 1890s. She died in New London of a stroke (cerebral apoplexy) on her seventy-eighth birthday (1897). We believe she was visiting her niece Mary W. Salter. Rufus Jr. had Winnie's body transferred to Nantucket for internment alongside those of her husband, Rufus; her young daughters; her aunt Sarah,; her mother, Anna B. Mitchell; and her stepfather, Frederick W. Mitchell, at the Prospect Hill Cemetery, Lot 68.

It is also unclear what type of financial or emotional support, if any, Frederick and his family received from their uncle, William H. Coffin, who lived in Providence, or from other relatives, like their aunts Mary, Abby, or Sarah, who were mentioned in letters. There were other relatives on the Parker family side, but it is not clear how involved they were. He had cousins from his aunt Mary Salter, although these lived in New Hampshire, Connecticut, or New York. His uncle William and cousins Jane and Gertrude lived in

39. A William Henry Coffin, age twenty-one, from Massachusetts, appears in the voter registration of California (Great Registers) on May 8, 1871. The registry showed him living at 23 Oak Grove Avenue in San Francisco.

Providence. And there were no first cousins on his mother's side on Nantucket, since she was an only child.

As noted earlier, the government denied Winnie's application for a pension in 1881. As a comparison, her sister-in-law, Abby Arnold, collected a pension upon the death of her husband, Richard Arnold, in 1882 of $20 per month ($532 in 2021), which the government increased to $50 ($1,400 in 2021) in 1885.

With the economic decline of the island, young Frederick may have felt no alternative but to seek better fortunes elsewhere. Perhaps he stopped with relatives as he looked for opportunities, like with his uncle William in Providence or his aunt Abby in Manhattan. Or perhaps he just sailed south. He left to never see his mother and brother in person again, al-though we believe there was some correspondence. There is no confirmation that Frederick may have gone first to California, although that is a possibility if his cousin William H. Lincoln may have been there. Stories about islanders heading to Texas—a new frontier after the Mexican-American War of 1847–1849—must have also seemed attractive. As a seaman, that must have been an easy trip, and he would have reached Mexico from the Gulf of Mexico. Northeast Mexico, unlike Nantucket, was a region that was experiencing an economic boom in the 1880s and 1890s with the construction of a national railway system.

And so ends Frederick's Nantucket chapter.

Frederick W. Mitchell (1794–1867), second husband of Annie Bunker Mitchell and stepfather of Winnie Chase Coffin. The photograph on the left is from the archives of the Nantucket Historical Association (C120). The illustration on the right is one of three belonging to the Quintanilla family that Frederick W. Coffin brought to Mexico.

A New Beginning South of the Border

We believe economic reasons motivated Frederick Coffin's departure from Nantucket. But let us not forget that his character may also have been molded by personal losses, a sense that his life could also be cut short, and perhaps a potentially overprotective mother. He disappears from local rosters and other island records by 1879. He likely sailed to Mexico and entered through the port of Veracruz in the Gulf of Mexico. It probably took him a couple of years to reach that port and get involved with the railroad construction. The first official records show him in Mexico in 1883.

There were widespread news reports about two growth industries at that time in both the United States and Mexico: mining and railroads. Mining has a long history of success in Mexico. As for railroads, the Mexican government granted the first concessions in the 1840s and 1850s to foreign investors. The first line that connected the port of Veracruz with Mexico City started operations in 1873.[40] President Porfirio Díaz initiated the construction of a modern rail network in full force in 1877. This construction program resulted in a sharp increase in Mexico's railway trackage, from seven hundred miles in 1880 to more than twelve thousand miles in 1900.

Frederick Coffin became involved with the National Railway, or Ferrocarril Nacional Mexicano, which started construction in 1881 and linked Mexico City to Nuevo Laredo, through San Luis Potosí, Saltillo, and Monterrey. The company was incorporated in Colorado in 1880. The Ferrocarril Nacional Mexicano reached Matamoros on the border with Texas in 1883 (we can place Frederick in San Luis Potosí that year) and provided that city with an important link to Central Mexico. In 1887, the government consolidated all individual construction concessions and reorganized the operating company

40. Three important lines in the railway network were built in the 1880s: Ferrocaarril Nacional (National Railway), linking Mexico City to Monterrey and Laredo through San Luis Potosí and Saltillo; Ferrocarril Central Mexicano (Central Railway), linking Mexico City to Nuevo León and later to El Paso at the US border, and the Pacific Coast port of Manzanillo through Guadalajara; and Ferrocarril Internacional Mexicano (International Railway), linking Piedras Negras at the US border with Torreon and the mining area of Durango.

as the Mexican National Railroad. It makes sense that Frederick would get involved with a growth enterprise at the time. He could pursue mining on the side, at least in the beginning.

The northeastern region of Mexico was among the poorest territories in the country until the second half of the nineteenth century.[41] Monterrey, founded in 1596, was no more than a village until the middle of the nineteenth century, surpassed by Puebla and León in Central Mexico. During the years of Spanish rule through 1821, Monterrey connected trade between San Antonio (Texas), Tampico on the Gulf coast, and Saltillo, San Luis Potosí, and the center of the country. Tampico's port brought many products from Europe, while Saltillo concentrated the trade between the northern territories and the country's capital city, Mexico City. San Antonio had been the key trade point with the northern foreign colonies (British and French).

After the Mexican War of Independence (1810–1821), Monterrey rose as a key economic center for the newly formed nation, especially because of its balanced ties between Europe (with its connections to Tampico), the United States (with its connections to San Antonio), and the capital (through Saltillo).

Monterrey developed as an important commercial and industrial center following the Mexican-American War. Because of the lost territories to the United States, the border came closer to the city and thereby tied Monterrey's fortunes to the Texas economy. The Civil War in the United States (1861–1865) also favored the formation of a regional capital. For instance, the cotton previously exported through the southern United States now passed through Monterrey

---

41. See Juan Mora-Torres, *The Making of the Mexican Border—The State, Capitalism, and Society in Nuevo León, 1848–1910* (Austin: University of Texas Press, 2001).

on its way to Europe. The French occupation (June 1864–July 1866) also caused important economic and political disruptions and nega- tively impacted those who had col- laborated with the Second Empire, especially the elite class.

In the late 1880s, Governor Bernardo Reyes granted signifi- cant concessions to industry, and important public works were undertaken during his adminis- tration, like the State Capitol and

Downtown Monterrey, ca. 1900

the water and drainage systems, wide avenues, and monuments. Monterrey truly took off in terms of the development of higher education, commerce, and industry. Widespread optimism was rampant, and the city was booming. Industry began to grow—glass, cement, beer, matches—with the explicit sup- port of several state administrations.

In 1880, Monterrey had its first industrial exposition. Moreover, the national railroad started operating with a link to Mexico City in 1881, with clear benefits to the local economy. Its population swelled from roughly four- teen thousand in 1850 to more than sixty thousand in 1900.

This is the operating environment that Frederick Coffin experienced when he arrived in the country. In 1883, Frederick Coffin lived in San Luis Potosí, probably because of this city's key position in the construction of the railroad line. Working for the railways allowed for extensive travel in the country, igniting his interest in mining, the other growth industry.

Although he was raised Presbyterian, in San Luis Potosí, he converted to Catholicism and was baptized on April 19, 1883. The priest came to his home to perform the ritual. The registry says that it was an "urgent" case, which we assume had to do with some form of illness. The family said that he had experienced a great illness at some point before his marriage but did not know any details. He was twenty-eight years old. His godparents were Ramón Mel- lado and Teresa Pedrajo. Priests performed this ritual at home in rare and isolated cases. Perhaps these individuals thought it was best he be baptized in the Catholic Church in case he might not recover.

Still, in the ensuing years, his work for the railroad company took him to other destinations. Some of these may have sparked his interest in mining and its potential riches. We do not believe he lived for an extended period in San Luis Potosí or Monterrey before or after his marriage in 1887. Frederick listed his primary residence as Saltillo, Coahuila, at that time. He lived around

Federico Coffin, Mexico, ca. 1885

Múzquiz, in the same state, following his marriage.

All these cities were undergoing significant change as the local economies were shifting. They were bustling with business activity, unlike the declining pace of Nantucket at the time. For instance, because of that island's economic slide, the last brick structure built there before the end of the century was the Coffin School building in 1852.

Frederick visited the mines at the town of La Esmeralda, in Sierra Mojada, Coahuila,[42] according to my father. We believe he met Juan Castillón[43] (1862–1946) at that location, who also lived for a while in that town. Juan was born in Monterrey, but he had strong roots in the neighboring state of Coahuila, and his ancestry dated back to the late 1770s to a village next to the Rio Grande.[44] Juan was married and mostly resided in that state. We understand that it was through Juan that Frederick (now called Federico) met his sister and future wife, Luisa.[45]

Luisa was the youngest of the adult Castillón daughters. She was born on July 17, 1867, and christened María Luisa two weeks later, on July 29. We believe Frederick must have been in towns that followed the railroad tracks in Coahuila or Nuevo León after he left San Luis Potosí in the mid-1880s. One of those trips brought him to Monterrey.

---

42. Sierra Mojada was founded in May 1879, following the discovery of silver in a mine, and it grew rapidly immediately afterward. This discovery must have been fresh in Frederick's mind in those early years of the town.

43. Castillón is a surname that originates in the Kingdom of Aragón and also in the south of France.

44. See appendix 1 for more information regarding the Castillón lineage.

45. In 1884, the principal settlements of the coal region were Múzquiz and San Juan de Sabinas. Also, in 1884, the first coal mining companies were established in this region to facilitate the industrial development in the country. For such, railroads were also required to help with the transportation of coal within Mexico and for export to Texas. See Rosalia Chavez, "El Ferrocarril Internacional y su Centralidad en el Nacimiento de la Cuenca Carbonífera de Coahuila (1866–1900)," *Mirada Ferroviaria* 9, no. 3 (2004): 13–21.

According to family lore, Frederick saw Luisa from his horse and said to himself, "I will marry her." He was just shy of thirty-two years of age, and she was twenty when they married in Monterrey on Saturday, August 20, 1887. The civil ceremony[46] took place at her home at Colegio de las Niñas #48 at 6:00 a.m. (today the street name is Francisco Javier Mina). Witnesses included Bernardino Lozano, Santiago Zambrano, and Dr. Desiderio Garza.

The civil registration of intention to marry lists his occupation as an employee of the Ferrocarril Nacional Mexicano (Mexican National Railroad),[47] while their religious marriage certificate lists his residence in neighboring Saltillo, Coahuila. Santiago Zambrano and Joaquín Castillón signed as witnesses of the religious ceremony.

Consuelo Coffin, Monterrey, 1892

Importantly, Frederick did inform his family back in Nantucket about his wedding to Luisa. And it got recorded in Eliza Starbuck Barney's journal with all Coffin descendants.

After their wedding, Frederick and Luisa initially settled in the town of Múzquiz, Coahuila. This town was home to many Castillón cousins. A first daughter was born there—Anita Luisa Coffin-Castillón—on May 11, 1888, nearly nine months after their wedding day. She was undoubtedly named after his deceased grandmother, Annie B. Mitchell, and sister, Annie M. Coffin. Sadly, she died twenty-six days later, on June 6, of a fever related to an "undetermined illness." This premature death may have triggered in him the

46. The state does not officially recognize religious ceremonies as binding for government official business after Mexico's Constitution of 1857. Therefore, church baptisms, marriages, and burials need to be separately accompanied by the civil registration of birth, marriage, and death. There is a complete separation of church and state, and that is why both types of records exist in Mexico since the early 1860s.

47. Jacobo Villalobos, one of my other great-grandfathers on my mother's side, was the railway's legal counsel in San Luis Potosí at the same time. Frederick and Jacobo may have crossed paths in San Luis Potosí in the 1880s.

Consuelo Coffin, Luisa Castillón, and Ana Coffin, ca. 1900

hidden pain of his deceased sisters. A second daughter—my grandmother—was born one year later on June 29, 1889, in the neighboring town of San Juan de Sabinas, an important coal mining center. Her parents baptized her María Consuelo at the local parish in Monclova, a neighboring town, on July 19, 1889. Her godparents were Melchor and Isabel Lobo. Her parents named my grandmother Consuelo after their first daughter died, as "consolation" for the death of their firstborn.

We ignore how long they stayed in that area because a third daughter, Ana Luisa, was born on July 8, 1891, in Monterrey.[48] Frederick pursued his mining interests, while Luisa moved with the girls back to Monterrey to be close to her mother. There is no record that Winnie, Frederick's mother, heard about her two granddaughters in Mexico. However, it was probable that he wrote to her about these births as he had about his marriage.

My father remembered frequent visits from his great-uncle Juan to Monterrey when he was a young child and receiving big silver coins from him. Despite her few memories, my grandmother recalled some stories her mother related. For instance, she recalled Frederick's intense passion for fine horses and metals. Today, he would have probably loved cars.

She also told stories about how her father was in awe of mountains (naturally, as Nantucket is flat), always thinking that those same mountains hid treasures and wealth deep inside them, waiting for someone to discover them. Of several stories, one in particular was especially remembered. It related to Frederick's failed attempt to get his wife, Luisa, to pull the trigger of a pistol by leaning on the head of his favorite horse.

My grandmother would show my father a few old photographs and illustrations dear to her father over time. She treasured these items and kept them

---

48. We found a christening record for Consuelo in the city of Monclova. Luisa obtained a civil certificate of birth for both surviving girls in Monterrey, issued on June 24, 1892.

in a small trunk in the large armoire in her bedroom, always close to her.[49] These few items were valuable enough for her father to carry to Mexico and for her to hang on to like precious gold. My father, as a little boy, admired these items in wonder, as they were enshrouded in mystery about a remote and unfamiliar land.

In any event, the family believed that Frederick died sometime in the early 1890s when the girls were too young to have vivid memories of him. And, slowly, his memory became only that—a memory. As Consuelo grew older, she increasingly looked more and more like Frederick. Luisa managed to raise the girls with income as a seamstress, complemented with financial help from her brothers, Juan and Alberto.

Luisa never married again, even though she was quite young and attractive.

Ana Coffin, ca. 1906

Consuelo and her sister Ana studied to become schoolteachers at the Escuela Normal Miguel F. Martinez. Consuelo obtained her degree in 1907. She was eighteen years old. That school was always dear to her throughout her life, and she formed long-lasting relationships with a few women of her class, who became secondary relatives to my father and his siblings. She taught at an elementary school (Escuela Simón de la Garza Melo on Diego de Montemayor Street), a noble profession for young ladies at the turn of the century.

With her sister Ana, she also taught for some time in the village of Villaldama, near Monterrey. Ana, nineteen, registered her intention to marry Jorge González-Villarreal (age twenty-seven) on September 23, 1910, in Villaldama. This engagement fell through, and Ana eventually married Jesús María Villarreal (age thirty-eight) in November 1913.[50] We believe her first fiancée married someone else in 1914. Their first son, Mario, died of chickenpox at three months of age on February 19, 1915. A second baby, Berta, also died at ten months of age in February 1916. Finally, their third child, Ana María,

49. Pedro F. Quintanilla Coffin, *El Mar, Mi Abuelo y Yo* (Monterrey, NL: Hojas Sueltas—Tomo II, 1984): 343–47.

50. We found a civil registration of marriage for Jorge González and Lilia Dueñez in December 1914.

Consuelo Coffin, 1907

was born on November 3, 1917. Sadly, Ana died a few weeks later on November 18. She was only twenty-five years old.[51]

Ana María grew up to be a rebellious teenager and became estranged from the rest of the family in the late 1930s, probably as a result of her father's second family. She moved to a border town and married a divorced customs agent in 1946, Bernardo Garcia, in Reynosa, Tamaulipas. She gave birth to five daughters between 1948 and 1956 in Cameron County, Texas. She died in 1963 in Matamoros. She was forty-five years old.

Consuelo married Galdino P. Quintanilla, a lawyer, on Thursday, February 1, 1912. The civil ceremony was held at 5 de Mayo #182 at ten o'clock in the morning. She was twenty-three years old, while he was about to turn thirty. Witnesses included her second cousin once removed Lic. Eugenio F. Castillón,[52] Lic. Secundino Roel, Lic. Antonio de la Paz Guerra, Lázaro Garza Ayala, Juan Castillón, and Eleuterio de la Garza. Both of Galdino's parents were deceased. Consuelo was getting married just as her Coffin first cousins back in Boston were babies. But who knew?

Frederick faded into oblivion. The family had moved on. There is very little information about Frederick during his short life in Mexico. As quickly as he appeared, he disappeared. Because he was a railroad employee, Frederick must have known well the villages and towns along the railroad track route.

---

51. Jesús María Villarreal went on to have an out-of-wedlock relationship with Luisa Villarreal in Candela, Coahuila, and had at least seven children with her, starting in 1920. They eventually married in 1932. He died in 1942, at age sixty-seven.

52. There are photographs of Eugenio F. Castillón in *Nuevo León: Imagenes de Nuestra Memoria*, Vol. II (Monterrey, NL: Consejo de la Cultura y las Artes de Nuevo León, 2004), 26 (his own wedding in 1884), 115, and 123. According to Israel Cavazos Garza, *Breve Historia de Nuevo León* (Mexico City, Mexico: El Colegio de Mexico, 1995), 193, he hosted President Venustiano Carranza at his home when he visited Monterrey on June 25, 1914.

Galdino P. Quintanilla-Garza and Consuelo Coffin-Castillón, Monterrey, Nuevo León, February 1, 1912

That explains his interest in mining and prospecting in new sites in the states of Coahuila and Durango. His friend and later brother-in-law Juan may have influenced him, as he was doing the same.

His death appears to have been sudden, and either there was no information to talk about within our family or his presence would have rather been forgotten. In any case, all contact with Nantucket (or Boston) and any Coffin relatives was then lost with his death.

Life in the Early 1900s

Both young Coffin women were able to make a life without their father's support. They studied and married in the early 1910s. However, only Consuelo survived to the end of the decade. She had married into a family with a long lineage in the north of Mexico and one that dated back to the early days of the Spanish conquest in the New World. This lineage can be traced back nearly eighty years before the *Mayflower* even landed in Massachusetts.[53]

Consuelo's husband, Galdino, was a lawyer who earned great professional respect in Monterrey. He was born on April 18, 1882, the eighth of ten children of Pedro Pablo Quintanilla and Guadalupe Garza y Garza.[54] Galdino's father had been an important industrialist and entrepreneur at a time when Monterrey's industry was taking off. He had businesses in silk manufacturing, matches, cornstarch, and starch, among others. Published records note that he was the most important industrialist of the era, not because of his financial success but because of "his strong spirit for enterprise and the tenacity he would place in his negotiations."[55] He was a multifaceted individual whose businesses collapsed once he died in 1906, because there was no one trained to take over from him. His sons all chose to be professionals in medicine, law, and education rather than in business. And his daughters were either teachers or housewives.

The state of Nuevo León suffered great political turmoil during the years in which Galdino studied law.[56] President Porfirio Díaz appointed Governor Reyes, and he had been reelected continuously for twenty years. In the early 1900s, the law school counted only about twenty-two students, most of whom

---

53. See appendix 2 for more information on the Quintanilla lineage.

54. Her name was María Guadalupe de la Garza y de la Garza.

55. See S. A. Porrúa De C. V., *Diccionario Porrua, Historia, Biografía y Geografía de México, 2nd edición* (Mexico City, Mexico: Editorial Porrúa, 1965), 1277.

56. He studied at the Colegio Civil and Escuela de Jurisprudencia de Nuevo León. He also published in the newspapers *Renacimiento*, *Redención*, and *Constitución*.

were idealistic and later became leaders of the community.[57] He was one of the student leaders during the uprising against Governor Bernardo Reyes on April 2, 1903, who had him arrested and jailed with others.

After the law school lifted his suspension, Galdino finally obtained his law degree in 1907, a year after his father's death, and soon thereafter the country itself was immersed in the revolution. His mother, Lupe, died in 1910. The city alternated being taken by conflicting armed forces during those years.

One of his classmates was Cecilio Garza-González, who later left for Mexico City and, in the mid- to late 1910s, became involved in national politics with

Galdino P. Quintanilla, Pedro F. Quintanilla, and Consuelo Coffin, 1915

Miguel Gómez-Noriega, my mother's father. Through this tie, my parents met in 1940.

It was during the 1910s that Galdino became a key member of the bar (at one point he was its president) and a faculty member of the law school. Education was so important to him that when the school closed because of political unrest, he (and others) would teach at their offices or in their homes. He also became very much involved in local politics. In fact, because of his politics, he ended up in jail for a short time in Monterrey around 1915 or 1916.

He was one of the legal intellectuals who wrote the new state constitution of 1917 and was also elected as a local state representative in several much-contested elections held that year. He became dean of the law school at the State University from 1925 to 1930. In 1931, Galdino insisted on reopening the debate about the legal labor rights of women when the state legislature started its session. As a result, the law was changed to give equal rights to

57. My mother's uncle Jacobo Villalobos-Reyes (1880–1944) from San Luis Potosí also studied law in Monterrey and married in this city in 1901. It is possible that they may have known each other.

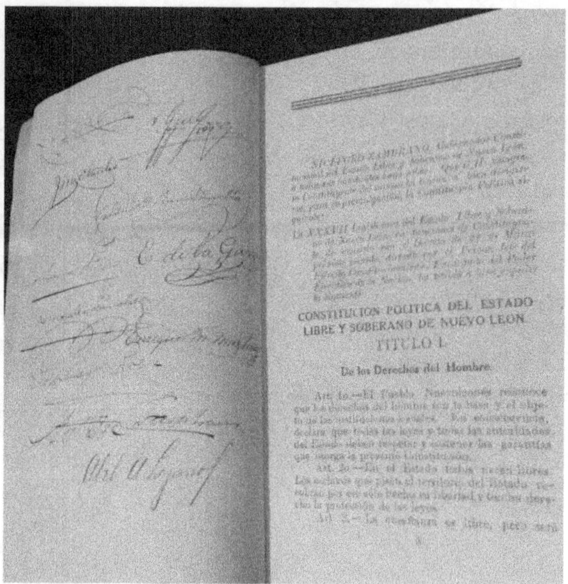

Signed Constitution of the state of Nuevo León, Museo
del Palacio de Gobierno, Monterrey

women in the workforce, Nuevo León being the first state in Mexico to do
so.[58] Strong ethics and morals motivated him, not money.

Galdino Quintanilla and Consuelo Coffin had seven children:

1. Pedro Francisco, my father, was born on October 4, 1914. He married
   Maria Josefina Gómez-Noriega (1917–1979) on July 17, 1943, in Mexico City. He died on November 10, 1992, at age seventy-eight, of an
   embolism and thrombosis. She died in 1979, at age sixty-one, from heart
   disease.
2. Galdino Federico died on August 5, 1916, when he was one month old—
   and two weeks after his uncle Joaquín died. He was the only child to have
   Federico as a middle name, a name never used again in our family.
3. Consuelo was born on December 8, 1918. She died of typhoid fever on
   October 30, 1937, just shy of her nineteenth birthday.
4. Raúl Alberto was born on October 23, 1919. His parents gave him his
   middle name after Luisa's younger brother. He never married. He studied
   law and became a notary public, achieving great success in his own right.
   He died on April 24, 1984, of a stroke, at age sixty-four.

---

58. *Historia de la Facultad de Derecho y Criminologia de la UANL, 1824–2002* (Monterrey, NL:
Universidad Autonoma de Nuevo León), 2003.

5. Maria Teresa was born on November 16, 1921. She probably was named after her mother's cousin Teresa Castillón. She never married. She passed away on January 4, 1988, of lung cancer (even though she was never a smoker), at age sixty-six.
6. Gabriela Guadalupe was born on February 27, 1924. My father named her. She married Eduardo Canseco (1912–2008) on May 3, 1947. She passed away on December 31, 2017, at age ninety-three.
7. Beatriz Enedina was born on May 14, 1927. Probably named after Consuelo's aunt Beatriz Castillón (Juan's wife). She died on January 22, 1986, of a heart attack. She married Carlos Ballí (1925–1999) on April 3, 1956. He remarried and died at age seventy-three.

The 1930s were difficult years worldwide because of the global economic Depression, and Monterrey was not immune to it. Also, the student riots and strikes at the State University forced my father to move to Mexico City to complete his law studies. In the 1930s, my grandfather bought land in Santa Catarina, next to Monterrey. He probably did not realize his family's history in that location. Every Sunday he would take his family to the *huerta* (orchard), and my grandmother would cook big meals for family and friends.

As the 1930s ended, Luisa Castillón died of "general weakness" in February 1939 at age seventy-one. With her passing, firsthand knowledge about Frederick Coffin was lost. A decade later a few of her friends told my grandmother that my brother resembled her father, which delighted her. A few years later, Galdino P. Quintanilla died in April 1943 of an aortic atheroma. He was sixty-one years old. Consuelo's years of widowhood were tough, but the silver lining was the grandchildren who began to fill her home. Consuelo Coffin died in September 1956, at age sixty-seven, from complications due to diabetes. Mexico's Coffin direct lineage thus ended. Frederick Coffin faded even more after her death.

Pedro F. Quintanilla-Coffin and Luisa Castillón, 1916

Front row: Raul, Maria Teresa, Consuelo, Beatriz, and Gabriela
Back row: Pedro F., Consuelo Coffin, and Galdino P. Quintanilla, Monterrey, ca. 1930

Standing: Beatriz E., Raul A., and Gabriela G., Monterrey, Nuevo León, 1938
Seated left to right: Pedro F., Consuelo Coffin, Galdino P. Quintanilla, Maria Teresa

Finally, the Truth

For decades, there was mystery surrounding Frederick Coffin. Slowly those who had met him passed away, and no one was certain as to where, when, or how he died. Nobody knew anything about his background and family. Our research into Frederick Coffin finally took a significant twist in the spring of 2010, when, by mere chance, we came across some newly accessible records.

April 8, 1895, was a warm Monday following Palm Sunday in Monterrey, just as the religious festivities associated with Holy Week were beginning. Luisa Castillón had not heard from her husband since shortly after the birth of their third daughter, Ana, in 1891. Nor had she received any financial support from him during those years. She was a young, struggling mother of two, only twenty-seven years old.

Luisa gathered enough courage to put an end to what had been a troubled relationship when she learned her husband was in town. She took the extraordinary step for a woman of her social standing at that time: She filed for divorce. This was not easy for women at the end of the nineteenth century in Mexico, as society frowned upon divorce, which was thought of as a scandalous practice that disrupted the cultural norm and the fabric of family relations. Women from the lower classes mainly initiated it, not women of Luisa's solid

Luisa Castillón, Monterrey, 1895

middle-class background.[59] But Luisa decided to defy convention and showed extreme strength of character and determination for a young woman. In the end, the fear of losing her daughters to her husband won over the negative association of being divorced. She was terrified and put a lot of thought into taking that step.

Someone had spotted Frederick at a local hotel and immediately told Luisa. She worried about Frederick taking their young daughters away. Her divorce filing eloquently put forth her case to the court: that her husband, whom she had married in 1887, "had abandoned her and their two young daughters since early 1892; that her husband had no real reason to leave her other than drunkenness or unkindness; and that his abandonment had resulted in his forfeiting his rights over her and their daughters, which she was petitioning the court to terminate."

She further noted that "it was she who had suffered from his drunkenness, which led him to be unbearably cruel towards her." In her filing, she mentioned that Frederick Coffin had written her in April 1892 from somewhere in Durango, Mexico, to let her know that he would be sending her half of his earnings and that he did not drink anymore, and he asked that she send him the few clothes he had left behind. Luisa had not heard from him since then, regardless of his promise of funds, nor had he provided any financial support for their young children. His abandonment, if truth be told, "had been absolute and notoriously unwarranted." So ended her emotional plea for a legal dissolution of her marriage.

Luisa proceeded to describe at great length "their sad situation and that it was thanks to her elderly mother and her brothers, Juan and Alberto, that they had not perished from hunger." She claimed that she had written Frederick several times about their living conditions but that "he had remained hard of heart, unmoved by the love of their daughters or by the generosity of her family which had taken care of his obligations, nor had he shown any consideration towards her." She had never given him a reason to regret his decision to marry her, as she had maintained it always pure as corresponded to "her honor, her character, and her family."

She wished that such a distressing situation not go on forever and found it "unfair that he would have rights over her and their daughters when he had relinquished them with his desertion." His presence in town presented thus the opportunity for her to "demand justice in the form of her divorce from him being granted by the courts and his rights correspondingly terminated."

This filing presents the rare opportunity to feel Luisa's anguish about the state of her marriage. However, the court did not resolve the matter because

59. See Sonia Calderoni, "Los Limites de lo Tolerable: El Divorcio en Nuevo León 1850–1910," in *Fondo Editorial Nuevo León* (Monterrey, NL: Archivo General del Estado de Nuevo León, 2008), Jueces de Letras, caja 698, año 1895.

Frederick needed to be served papers within nine days of the filing, and we are uncertain if he was served them. He may have left Monterrey knowing what was to happen, not seeing his family at all. Luisa was approaching twenty-eight years of age, and their daughters, Consuelo and Ana, were nearly six and three, respectively.

Luisa changed the story for the benefit of the family. It was not Frederick but his brother, Rufus, who had come to town looking for the girls to take them back to Boston. So she hid them from him. We now believe that she was in fact hiding them from their father, but it was easier to blame it all on Rufus. There is no record that Rufus ever came to Monterrey.

This was an extremely disturbing finding and one that nobody in the family knew about. I often wonder what my father would have thought of his grandfather abandoning his mother and aunt. I doubt that he would have had fond thoughts about the man whom he had sought information about all his life. A lifetime of mystery was thus revealed: the man had renounced his rights to even be remembered or his memory honored in any way.

The final discovery completed the search that began when I was a young man. On October 28, 2015, I retrieved Frederick's death certificate after decades of searching for it. He died four years after Luisa filed the papers for a divorce in 1895. The location was Mineral San Dimas in Durango, a remote, mountainous region in the western end of that state, near the border with the state of Sinaloa. According to the death certificate, he "died of poisoning that he alone caused himself" at the Mina La Candelaria on June 7, 1899, at 8.00 a.m.[60] The town clerk recorded the death the following day.

Reading between the lines, his death was no accident, no murder, and did not follow a prolonged illness. Alcohol poisoning could have been a possibility, although it is not clear. We know from Luisa's account that he was an alcoholic, much like his father, Rufus, may have been. He is described as a miner, and the region is well known for its rich deposits of gold, silver, and copper. There is no mention of his working for the railroad company in the death certificate.

It was a sad ending to a troubled and enigmatic life. San Dimas is a very remote place even today, with no paved roads into it from the state capital. He was given a third-class burial in the local cemetery, and the record mentions his marriage to "a lady from Monterrey" but of unknown name. It seems that two friends were the ones who dealt with his body and burial. And somehow the news did get to Luisa in Monterrey at some point.

Everything makes sense now. The Castillón family *intended* to erase any memory of Frederick W. Coffin. Luisa's widowhood left her in better social

---

60. Not 1898 as the Coffin Bible recorded it. Yet another example that his death was communicated to his brother in Boston, even if one year off.

standing than a divorce. Luisa found it easier to tell her daughters their father had died rather than abandoned them. The girls last saw their father when they were too young to have anything other than vague memories of him, even though his death occurred several years later. There were no family portraits, only of Luisa with her daughters. There was probably no family memory of his place of death, his date of death, or of any illness that caused his death. There was no more discussion about him in the family, as we speculate that Luisa preferred to keep the painful truth of their father's neglect away from her young daughters. It was less hurtful to say that he died in a distant place. Only very close family and Luisa's dear friends knew the truth, and those individuals respected her wishes, and that truth was eventually forgotten over time.

But now a long-standing and very well-kept family secret was finally exposed. And my mother had been right all along after all, although he did not leave Luisa for another woman.

He simply was a cad.

Frederick W. Coffin comes back to life as perhaps the black sheep. He enjoyed a privileged environment in his early days. But his youth was marred by tragedy, and he experienced much personal loss, ending his days possibly as an alcoholic like his father. But we can also speculate that he might have left Nantucket because of a more serious offense and not only a sense of adventure: his mother deeded their home solely to his brother in 1880, long before her death in 1897. Frederick was left out, either because he did not deserve it or because she recognized he would never come back.

Luisa's allegations that he was a drunkard and abusive, while possibly exaggerated as these situations typically are in legal filings, cannot hide the fact that he did not take care of his daughters, financially or emotionally. Consuelo had no memory of him, even though he died when she was ten years old. She thought she was younger than she was when she last saw him. And Consuelo grew up loving the idea of a father who did not really exist.

While keeping her secret well guarded while she lived, Luisa, in her divorce filing, reached beyond her grave and through time to set the record straight about her unkind husband.

We thus conclude our search for Frederick Coffin. The core of who Frederick was will remain a mystery forever, and we honor Luisa's wishes this way. Still, we are much enriched by the journey we took and the many findings of so many other ancestors and bloodlines, all of whom we can be proud of. As for "Freddy," Marcus Tullius Cicero should have added: "The life of the dead is placed in the memory of the living—*or in the writings of those who knew them well.*"

Epilogue

Nantucket offered no prospects of jobs in his foreseeable future, so Frederick Coffin had to choose between staying connected to his shriveling roots or risking everything to start a new life elsewhere. He chose the latter. And he undoubtedly had to make hard choices along his life's journey. The most important ones turned out to be bad choices. But perhaps he could not help himself.

As the search for one individual ends, we reflect on how much we learned about where he came from, what circumstances may have formed his character, when he died, and where he died.

Although the specific search for Frederick Coffin reached an end, this family story does not end. After two hundred years, a new generation of Quintanilla (and Coffin) descendants have formed families of their own. Some in Mexico, some in the United States. Old hands continue to touch new ones. New bloodlines and lineages are being added. Families continue to be disassembled and rearranged. Bloodlines, once very distinct and in separate geographies, have converged and expanded at the same time into the new millennium.

What started as the search for one individual became a journey across time, geographies, and lineages. So enriching, indeed. We have researched the Coffins of Massachusetts, the Castillóns and Sepúlvedas from Coahuila and Nuevo León, the Gómez-Noriegas from Sinaloa, and the Villalobos from Michoacán and San Luis Potosí, all blending with the Quintanillas from Nuevo León—and now the US. We have learned so much about so many of these individuals. Frederick Coffin did leave a legacy behind through his daughters, Consuelo and Ana. Each of them has abundant descendants both in the United States and in Mexico. All of them represent a success story in carrying forward their dreams and hopes, by forming their own families.

And it is now up to future generations to carry on with values, with history, and with stories for their children and grandchildren. It is looking into the future, one with optimism and dreams, that I finish this story, hoping that my children, nephews, nieces, and cousins will be able to add to it with their experiences and keep the story going. After all, the story is theirs to make.

Rodrigo Quintanilla, Daniela Quintanilla, Vivian Altman, and Julian Quintanilla, December 19, 2009

Appendix 1

As we noted earlier, we provide more background and detailed lineages for the Castillón and Quintanilla families in appendixes 1 and 2.

We trace the Castillón family line to the village of Mascota, Jalisco, which lies between Puerto Vallarta on the Pacific coast and Guadalajara, during the first half of the 1700s. At that time, Mascota was under the jurisdiction of Guachinango. Spanish conquistadors first came to this area in the mid-1520s, but mining drove the first Spanish settlements in this region in the 1540s. The Castillón individuals who we can find here engaged in both mining and agriculture. They owned lands at Hacienda Santa Rosa, and life events were registered at the village parish either in Mascota or Guachinango (Huachinango in church records).

We begin with Antonio Joseph Castillón, who married Ana Petra de la Peña sometime between 1746 and 1748. They had at least three sons who moved to the northern frontier: Vicente (about 1756–1785), Joaquín (about 1755–1812), and Onofre. We believe other children stayed nearby, including Juan Eugenio (about 1753–1799), Juan María, and Margarita.

Sometime in the mid-1750s, several sons moved to Real Presidio de San Juan Bautista del Rio Grande, now Guerrero (renamed in the 1820s after Vicente Guerrero, a hero of the Mexican fight for independence from Spain). Spaniards preferred the presidio as the instrument to expand the population to the northern frontier and to protect the new inhabitants from hostile Indians during the late 1600s and 1700s. They expected these settlements to become somewhat self-sufficient and grow in size and to offer a strong buffer against foreign invaders. Until then, the surrounding area on both sides of the Rio Grande had been occupied by small, mobile groups of hunters and gatherers. And there might have been economic incentives for the Castillón siblings to move to these new lands.

This part of northeastern Mexico has a very dry climate. In the past, freshwater springs termed *ojos de agua* emanated near present-day Guerrero, creating an oasis in the desertlike lands of Northern Coahuila. The springs carried a high charge of travertine in solution, and these deposits formed a natural dam sometime in the ancient past, creating a large lake (*laguna*) and a smaller lake behind it. Several fords (*pasos*) across the nearby Rio Grande made this locality particularly attractive to the Spanish.

From 1700 to 1716, San Juan Bautista was the most advanced outpost on the northeastern frontier of New Spain. San Juan Bautista was one of three missions and a presidio built in 1700. The other two were San Francisco Solano (March 1700) and San Bernardo (1702). The missions were situated in a triangular pattern around the important springs and lakes. Initially, the government assigned a mobile cavalry unit to protect the missions. San Juan Bautista's growth became stunted because the railroad bypassed it and was instead directed to Piedras Negras.[61]

Unfortunately, church records from the Real Presidio de San Juan Bautista are spotty and incomplete. Therefore, we cannot fill in the gaps that exist in relationships, births, marriages, or deaths of those first settlers from the Castillón family.

For instance, it is not clear who the eldest son was. Vicente married Teodora de la Garza at the Presidio around 1778, with whom he had at least five children: Jose Patricio (1779), Rosa Maria (1780), Jose Onofre (1783), Jose Miguel Francisco (1784), and Juan (1785). We did not find a baptism record for Juan, but we did find his death record on April 30, 1786, as a one-year-old, with his father, Vicente, deceased. This suggests Vicente was about thirty years old when he died.

Our research showed that our Castillón lineage lies with Joaquín Castillón (1755–1812). He married Clemencia Sáenz, also at the Presidio, on April 16, 1788, with whom he had at least eight children. Their marriage record indicates that Teodora de la Garza was a witness. We speculate that this was his widowed sister-in-law, who married his brother ten years earlier. The record states that he was also from Mascota, Jalisco, although no ages were provided for either Joaquin or Clemencia, nor was any information available about their parents. Joaquin died on June 10, 1812, and his age is quoted as being fifty-seven. Therefore, he would have been born around 1755 and married when he was thirty-three. Clemencia would have been much younger. Teodora also appears as baptism godmother to several of Joaquin and Clemencia's children.

Joaquin was fifty-four when their last child was born. Therefore, she must have been in her early forties at most when she gave birth to a child in 1809.

61. Taken from Gateway Missions from the University of Texas at Austin in Wikipedia. See also Luis Arnal, "El Sistema Presidial en el Septentrión Novohispano, Evolución y Estrategia de Poblamiento," *Scripta Nova: Revista Electrónica de Geografía y Ciencias Sociales* X, no. 218 (26) (2006): www.ub.es/geocrit/sn/sn-218-26.htm.

We estimate that she was born around 1770. Their children included the following:

1. José Irineo (1789–1849), who married María Genoveva Melo (1797–1855).
2. Juan María Trifón (1791–ca. 1850), who married Rafaela de la Garza (1801–1876).
3. José Dionisio (1793–1871), who married María Josefa Sánchez in 1823.
4. Albino (1794–1871), who married Dolores Melo (1797–1857).
5. Maria Petra (1797–1798). She died in infancy.
6. Juan Francisco Tirso (1800), who married María Josefa Parra.
7. Juan Mateo (1803–1881).
8. Juana Maria (1809).

Their descendants are numerous in Northeast Mexico and the United States. Juan María married Rafaela de la Garza, born in 1801, in 1820; he was twenty-eight, and she was nineteen years old. Juan María died around 1850. Juan Maria and Rafaela had a least seven children:

1. José de Jesús (1822–1908).
2. José Antonio (1823–1910).
3. Juan Nepomuceno (1828–1854), who married Rita Menchaca (1826–1854).
4. Manuel (1831–1889), who married Narcisa Sepúlveda (1834–1896) in 1853.
5. Tirso (1832–about 1880), who married Maria Alvina Hernández in 1853.
6. Rafael (1842–1906), who married Maria Ignacia Treviño in 1862.
7. Macario (1843–1894), who married Gertrudis Cano in 1873.

Given the large gap between Tirso and Rafael, we believe that there could have been more children born who died very young. We descend from Manuel.

Manuel moved to Monterrey sometime during his youth, where he met Narcisa Sepúlveda (1834–1896). He wed Narcisa in Ciudad Guadalupe's main church, on Sunday, November 6, 1853; he was twenty-three, and she was nineteen. His father, Juan Maria, was deceased by that time while his mother, Rafaela de la Garza, was still living.

Narcisa was born on October 28, 1834, in Hacienda La Laja, in what is now Ciudad Guadalupe. Hacienda La Laja was also known as Hacienda San Rafael de Tierra Dura, and its origins date back to the settlement of Monterrey in the late 1590s.

Her parents were Vicente Sepúlveda (1798–1858) and Francisca de la Garza, who had also wed at the Hacienda on August 12, 1820. Vicente's grandfather Juan-Vicente de Sepúlveda acquired the controlling interest of the Hacienda in the 1770s through his marriage to Margarita de la Garza.

Narcisa Sepúlveda, ca. 1890

It was a very large clan. Reports indicate that Juan-Vicente had eight children with his first wife and twenty more with his second!

Both Manuel and Narcisa were born when Texas and California were still part of Mexico. They were both teenagers at the time of the Mexican-American War and the city's occupation by the US Army during 1846 to 1848. Eventually, one of their daughters would marry a man from the country to the north.

The Castillón couple had fourteen children according to christening and death records, although we acknowledge a few of these records do not make any sense (unless some names were repeated because an older child died):

1. Rosa (1854–1931). She married Rufino Garza (1846–1893) in 1870. They had ten children, several of whom died in infancy.
2. Juan Maria (1856).
3. Juana (1856–1860). She died in infancy.
4. Manuel (1857). We assume he died in infancy.
5. A second Juana (1859).
6. A second Manuel (1860).
7. Juan Teódulo (1862–1946). He married his second cousin Beatriz Castillón in 1884. They had ten children. He lived in Múzquiz, Monclova; in Sierra Mojada; and finally in Torreón.
8. Juan Francisco (1863).
9. Twins Rafaela and Guadalupe (1866) died at two months old in October.
10. Luisa (1867–1939). She married Frederick W. Coffin in 1887. They had two daughters.
11. María de Jesús (1869) died at three months old in November.
12. Alberto (1871–1941). He married Carlota de la Garza (1881–1933) in 1903. They had six sons and moved to San Antonio, Texas.
13. Vicente Sixto (1872–1874). He died in infancy.

Parenthetically, Manuel Castillón also had at least one illegitimate child, Esteban, with Margarita Flores. This child died at the age of eight months on March 2, 1872. We do not know if Narcisa and his other children were aware of this child or whether there were others. They adopted a child named Juana, born in 1865, who married Anselmo Garcia from Aguascalientes, at age twenty-nine, on January 25, 1880. For all we know, this child could also have been illegitimate.[62]

It appears that the only ones who reached adulthood were Rosa, Juan Teódulo, Luisa, and Alberto, and these four had issue. We have little information about descendants from Juan and Alberto, although we know her two brothers were important throughout Luisa's life.

Manuel Castillón died of pneumonia on September 7, 1889, at age fifty-seven, and Narcisa died of bronchitis six years later, on February 13, 1896, when she was sixty-one years old. Her death announcement places her address at Colegio de las Niñas 50. At the time of Narcisa's death, only her sister Maria Guadalupe Estefana survived her, other than her children.

62. We speculate that this Juana's husband, Anselmo, may have died soon after their marriage. There is a Juana in the birth records having an out-of-wedlock relationship with a Tomas Ramírez, shoemaker. She appears to have had at least seven children with him starting in 1885. Juana died on June 3, 1907.

Appendix 2

Quintanilla Ancestry

José Diego De Treviño (Abt. 1537-?)	Beatriz de Quintanilla (Abt 1539-Aft.1603)
Juan De Farias (Abt. 1554-Abt. 1612)	Maria Treviño de Quintanilla (1558-Abt.1620)
Lucas Garcia (Abt. 1574-1627)	Juliana de Quintanilla (Abt. 1578-Abt.1640)
Bartolome Gonzalez Olivares (1598-1672)	Ana Garcia de Quintanilla (Abt. 1620-1684)
Nicolas Gonzalez de Quintanilla (1655-1689)	Beatriz Fernandez (1655-1687)
Juan G. de Quintanilla Fernandez (1687-Abt. 1750)	Maria Saenz (1700-Abt.1760)
Juan Diego de Quintanilla (1717-1788)	Antonia Margarita Garcia (1721-1801)
Jose Domingo Quintanilla (1747-Bef.1810)	Maria Antonia Guerra (1746-1810)
Juan Joseph Quintanilla (1778-1835)	Juana Rodriguez (1785-1850)
Jose Cayetano Quintanilla (1803-1864)	Dorotea Garcia Padilla (1817-1882)
Pedro P. Quintanilla (1837-1906)	Guadalupe Garza y Garza (1850-1910)
Galdino P. Quintanilla (1882-1943)	Consuelo Coffin (1889-1956)

The Quintanilla name has a long tradition in Northern Mexico. We believe Beatriz de Quintanilla is the first individual with that surname born in the New World. She was born about 1539 in Mexico City, allegedly to Sephardic parents, Bartolomé de Quintanilla and Juliana Farías, who arrived in New Spain in the 1530s.[63]

Few records, if any, exist about Beatriz. Beatriz married José Diego de Treviño (also Tremiño)[64] in Mexico City in 1557. He was born around 1537 in Spain. His parents, Diego Tremiño de Velasco and Francisca de Alcocer Bañuelos, had married in Seville and departed for the New World on June 13, 1538. Although they had first decided to go to Colombia, they settled in Mexico. Besides Diego, Maria Ana, Francisca, and Baltasar traveled with them.

The Treviño family moved to Guadalajara around 1543. Guadalajara had been initially founded in 1532, but its current location dates from 1542, its fourth settlement. The Spaniards expanded their search for silver and gold to the north and east once the Aztec empire was under their control. Baltasar de Treviño is credited with being one of the founders of the city of Zacatecas in the late 1540s, when he was in his late teens. Some records show that he claimed he was born around 1530. He remained in Zacatecas while his younger brother, José Diego, continued to Saltillo, which was founded in 1577.[65] José Diego finally settled in Monterrey after 1603 with his wife, mother, and other relatives.

Although most genealogists note that Beatriz died in 1572, in 1652, her grandson Diego de Ayala requested a marriage dispensation to marry Margarita de Sosa y Saldivar, daughter of his second cousin Maria de Sosa. In it, he mentions that his grandfather José de Treviño entered Monterrey in 1603 with his wife, Leonor de Ayala, and his mother, Beatriz de Quintanilla. Therefore, his father, José Diego, must have died before 1603 and Beatriz after 1603.[66]

Historians note that José Diego and Beatriz had at least nine children:

1. María was born on March 26, 1558, in Mexico City. After her first husband died, María married her second husband, Juan de Farías (ca. 1554– ca. 1612) around 1575 in Mazapil, Zacatecas. He was born in Portugal (he was known as Juan the Portuguese), and Juan and Maria were among

63. Many Jews who converted may have chosen to come to the New World, particularly sparsely populated Northern Mexico, to practice Judaism secretly without the oversight of the government and the Catholic Church.

64. Jose Diego de Treviño (also Tremiño) appears to be a descendant of High Chamberlain Pedro Fernandez de Velasco, First Count of Haro, born about 1395 and died in 1470 in Spain.

65. María Elena Santoscoy Flores, *Aquellos Primeros Saltillenses* (Saltillo, Mexico: Gobierno Municipal de Saltillo, 2012).

66. Sagrada Mitra de Guadalajara, Antiguo Obispado de la Nueva Galicia, #2885, page 574. Sagrada Mitra de Guadalajara. Rollo 168604 OAH 3028, Matrimonios Hojas Sueltas, Siglo XVII, 1638–1699, 3a Serie. 21 de enero de 1653. María de la Luz Montejano Hilton.

the early settlers of Saltillo.[67] Their children included Juliana, Sebastiana, Alonso, Ana, Martín Sánchez, Juan *"el mozo"* (the younger) de Farías, and José de Farías.

2. Isabel was born on November 12, 1562, in Mexico City. She married Pedro de Salazar, with whom she had Juana María Isabel and Ana de Salazar.
3. Joseph was born on March 22, 1565, in Mexico City. He married Leonor de Ayala Valverde. They had Francisco, Juan, Joseph, Alejo, Diego de Ayala, Ana, and Leonor de Treviño. José and Leonor settled in Monterrey in 1603.
4. Juana was born in 1566. She married Marcos Alonso de la Garza Falcón from Lepe, Huelva, Andalucía, Spain. They had ten children.[68]
5. Francisco was born in 1569.
6. Baltasar was born in 1571.
7. Diego was born in 1572.

Genealogists assert that they were all born in Mexico City. The younger ones, however, may have been born in a different town as they journeyed north toward Saltillo. For instance, a common stop was the mining town of Mazapil (Zacatecas) along the "Silver Road."

67. Juan de Farias may have been related to María's maternal grandmother, Juliana Farias, as they were all "new" Christians. According to some records, Juan de Farias was born in Portugal around 1554. He probably was of Jewish descent. It is not known when he came to the New World. In 1603, he moved to Monterrey and received land grants by the plain near Topo. In 1604–1605, the governor appointed him "alcalde ordinario," and he became "alcalde mayor" from 1606 to 1612. In 1615, he moved to Saltillo and became "alcalde ordinario." They bequeathed their son Juan the hacienda Los Berros, south of Saltillo. Upon the elder Juan's death, his children went to Saltillo and sold their father's lands to Diego de Ayala in 1650. (footnote 47 in Valentina Garza Martinez and Juan Manuel Perez Zeballos, *Libro del Cabildo de la Villa de Santiago del Saltillo 1575–1655* [Mexico City, Mexico: Centro de Investigaciones y Estudios Superiores en Antropologia Social, 2002]).

68. The primogenitor of the de la Garza Falcón family was Capt. Marcos Alonso Garza y del Arcón, also known as Marcos Alonso Garza y del Arcón, a Spanish nobleman, native of Lepe, province of Huelva, Spain. He arrived in Mexico City about 1550, became very active in the Spanish court social circles, and married into the prominent Treviño family, also known as the Tremiño family. Her brother was General José de Treviño. In 1569, he and his wife arrived at the town of Guadiana, present-day Durango City, in the province of Nueva Viscaya, present-day state of Durango. Here two of his sons were born, Don Alonso de Treviño and Don Josef de Treviño. (Notice that the children took their maternal family name of Treviño, since the Treviño family was more prominent.) Capt. Marcos Alonso Garza y Arcón was a miner by trade, and he and his family arrived as settlers at Real del Mapimi, a mining town, in the province of Nueva Viscaya (Durango). His three other children, Don Pedro de la Garza, Dona Juana Treviño, and Don Blas de la Garza Falcon, were born at Real del Mapimi. In 1603, his brother-in-law Gen. José de Treviño encouraged Don Marcos Alonso and his grown-up family to move to the Hacienda de San Francisco in the jurisdiction of Monterrey, Nuevo León, México. His two sons, Don Alonso and Don Blas, bought the hacienda. After his wife's death, Don Marcos Alonso de la Garza married Doña Catalina Martinez Guajardo, and two daughters, Dona Juana de la Garza and Dona Isabel Martinez, were born from this matrimony. (Notice that Isabel Martinez took her maternal family name.) His daughters married into prominent Nuevo León families, who contributed to the settlement of the new province of Nuevo Santander and the pacification of the Indians. (From Clotilde P. Garcia, *Captain Blas María de la Garza Falcón: Colonizer of South Texas* [Austin, TX: San Felipe Press, 1984]).

The governor appointed Juan de Farías mayor of Monterrey and later of Saltillo. In those days, some children took their father's surnames, while others opted to take on their mother's.[69] This may have been related to children choosing the surname perhaps least associated with Sephardic Jews to better take advantage of privileges available to new settlers.

Two daughters of Juan and María, Sebastiana and Juliana, married brothers Diego Rodríguez (ca. 1570–ca. 1625) and Lucas García (ca. 1576–ca. 1627) and settled in Monterrey. They were sons of Portuguese Baltasar Castaño de Sosa, a founder of Saltillo. Baltasar was also the son-in-law of Diego de Montemayor (1530–1611), the principal founder of Monterrey in 1596.[70]All of them were from Sephardic Jewish backgrounds. Historical records are sketchy, but by most accounts, Lucas García was Diego de Montemayor's grandson through his daughter Inés Rodríguez (from his first wife of the same name).

Shortly after the founding of Monterrey, Lucas García and Juliana de Quintanilla received title to farming land in Santa Catarina in November 1596, west of Monterrey.[71] They named this settlement Estancia de Santa Catarina, a resting place on the road to Saltillo. Santa Catarina did not officially become a village until the second half of the nineteenth century. People referred to Lucas as "Captain of the Peace" because of his fluency in indigenous languages. *Cacique Huajuco* and a band of Indians burned down their home in May 1624, and the original grant documents were lost. The governor later confirmed the land grant to his widow, Juliana, in 1635. There are numerous written accounts of the early days of the settlement of Coahuila, Texas, and Nuevo León, all of which provide great detail about family interrelationships as well as commercial and land dealings among these early settlers. Inbreeding was so prevalent that Lucas García used to boast that he was related to all settlers of these lands.

69. In some instances, the practice followed the Portuguese custom of the mother's last name first and the father's second. Many of these settlers hailed from Portugal. Only through other sources, like wills and testaments or marriage dispensations, can family relationships be clarified.

70. Alberto del Canto founded a village called Santa Lucía in what is now Monterrey in 1577, but the settlement never took hold. Luis Carvajal y de la Cueva made a second attempt at a settlement in 1582, but it was also unsuccessful. Finally, Diego de Montemayor founded the city in 1596 with thirteen families from Saltillo. Diego de Montemayor had three wives (Inés Rodríguez, María de Esquivel, and Juana Porcalla de la Cerda) and a legitimate child with each one (Inés, Diego, and Estefanía, respectively). He killed his third wife, Juana Porcalla, when he confronted her for having an affair with Alberto del Canto, founder of Saltillo, who became his archenemy. His third child with Juana, Estefanía, later married Alberto del Canto, her mother's lover, and had at least three children with him who survived to adulthood: Diego, Elvira, and Maria. These children all took the surname Montemayor.

71. Santa Catarina today is part of Monterrey's metropolitan area.

Lucas and Juliana had at least ten children:[72]

1. Diego was born in 1601. He married Mariana de Saldívar de Sosa in 1629, with whom he had six children: Josepha, Diego, Vicente de Saldívar, Pedro, Thomas, and Gaspar.
2. Bernardo was born in 1605. He married Maria Saldívar de Sosa, supposedly in 1653. They had at least one son, Pedro García de Sosa.
3. Bartolomé was born in 1615.
4. Lucas was born in 1617. He married Josefa de Ayala in 1667, a second cousin, and they needed a dispensation. They had Nicolás, Ana, María, and Lucas.
5. Beatriz was born in 1618. She never married. In her last will, she left her possessions to her siblings Thomas and Ana. She died in 1672.
6. Juana was born in 1619. She married Nicolás Flores.
7. Ana was born in 1620. She married Bartolomé Olivares González (1598–1672) in 1643, with whom she had Joseph Diego, Bartolomé, Nicolás, Joseph, Ana, and Antonio. She died in 1684.
8. Nicolás was born in 1624. He married Juana de Bracamonte in 1668. Their children included Juliana, Juan, Alonso, and Thomas.
9. María de la O[73] was born in 1625. She married José de la Cruz. On May 4, 1686, she sold her share of her inheritance (in land and horses) from her parents to her nephew Barlolomé Gonzalez de Quintanilla in 200 pesos in *reales*. She stated being in dire need, given that her husband had departed ten years prior for Real del Sombrerete and left her with a daughter.
10. Thomás was born in 1626. He first wed Isabel de Arredondo, and after her death, he married María de la Garza Falcón in 1684, herself the widow of Capt. Diego de Ayala. They had to get dispensation because of their blood relationship. Some records say he was fifty years of age in 1684, which would place his birth in 1634 and not 1626. But his father had died around 1627, so that record cannot be accurate. Maria's grandfather was Capt. Blas de la Garza, who was Juliana de Quintanilla's first cousin, mother of Thomás. On Thomás father's side, Maria's father, Lázaro de la Garza, was the son of Petronila de Montemayor, daughter of Capt. Miguel de Montemayor, who married Monica Rodríguez, daughter of Diego Rodriguez, brother of Thomás's father, Capt. Lucas García. Also, Thomás's first wife, Isabel, was the first cousin of Monica Rodríguez, Maria's grandmother. Maria's first husband, Gen. Diego de Ayala, had been Juliana de Quintanilla's first cousin. In light of these relationships, they got dispensation for their marriage, which the church granted in Guadalajara on March 6, 1684. With María de la Garza Falcón Montemayor (1654–1698) he had Petronila, Juan José Francisco, and Christóbal. He died in 1697.

Research of those early years of expansion into the northeast frontier has been growing over time, but it remains sparse. To be sure, family interrelationships

72. There is disagreement in birth years since their records are not available.
73. Francisco Sepúlveda Garcia, *Cronología de Santa Catarina* (La Fama, NL: Nogales, 1999).

among these Spaniards remained very tight, possibly because of their Sephardic background. As in New England in the 1700s, there are a lot of intermarriages among certain families, so last names are constantly being repeated. And church dispensations for marriages had to be requested.

Ana García de Quintanilla (ca. 1620–1684)[74] married widower Bartolomé Olivares González (1598–1672) around 1643. Ana was his third wife. He arrived in Monterrey a few years earlier from what today is the state of Hidalgo in Central Mexico to benefit from the pacification and settlement of Mexico's northeast frontier region.[75] He was originally from Morón de la Frontera (close to Seville), Andalucía, Spain. Bartolomé became one of the roots for the González surname in Northeast Mexico and South Texas.[76]

Bartolomé and Ana had at least five children:

1. José Diego (1645–1710), who married María de Ochoa Elizalde in 1671 and had six children. He used González as the principal surname, and so did his descendants.
2. Bartolomé (1652–1713), who married Nicolasa Fernández de la Garza (1650–1725) in 1672 and had eight children. Nicolasa was a third cousin. He also used González de Quintanilla and became an important branch for the González surname in the region.
3. Nicolás (1656–1688), who married Beatriz Fernández de Tijerina (1655–1687) in 1675 and had Nicolás, Ana Nicolasa, Gregorio, Miguel, and Juan. Beatriz was the sister of Nicolasa and also a third cousin. He and his offspring used G. de Quintanilla, so Quintanilla became the dominant surname for his descendants.
4. José (1658–?).
5. Ana (?–1699). She married Bernabé de la Garza.

The church registries abbreviate such that Nicolás González de Quintanilla became Nicolás G. de Quintanilla, and every descendant after him is either registered de Quintanilla or simply Quintanilla. To our knowledge, not much has been researched, however, about the Quintanilla lineage that

74. Some genealogical references point to 1625 as her birthdate, but we think this implausible, since her mother would have been close to fifty years old at her birth. Other birth years for Ana's siblings seem to be after the recorded death of their father, Lucas Garcia, which also does not make any sense.

75. Bartolomé was a widower, having first married Catalina González (perhaps in Spain) and Isabel Gómez de Esquivel in Tepetitlán, Hidalgo. We believe they had four children together: Andres (1631), Diego (1634), Maria (1637), and Isabel (1640). His wife, Isabel, seems to have died in 1640, perhaps because of the last child she bore. He then moved to the Monterrey area in the north and married Ana Garcia de Quintanilla, with whom he fathered at least five more children.

76. See Carl Lawrence Duaine, *With All Arms: A Study of a Kindred Group* (Austin, TX: Nortex Press, 1987); Guillermo Garmendia Leal, *Los Gonzalez de Nuevo Leon* (Hidalgo, TX: FamilySearch International, 1995); and Joel Rene Escobar y Saenz, *Capt. Bartolome Gonzalez and His Descendants* (Pharr, TX: J. R. Escobar, 2005).

can be traced back to Ana de Quintanilla through her son Nicolás. Perhaps these siblings taking on different surnames has created some confusion.

Nicolás and Bartolomé, sons of Bartolomé and Ana, married sisters Beatriz Fernández de Tijerina and Nicolasa Fernández de la Garza in 1675 and 1672, respectively. They were third cousins between them: the men's grandmother Juliana de Quintanilla was a first cousin of the women's grandfather Blas de la Garza y Falcón. All four of them had common great-great-grandparents: José de Treviño and Beatriz de Quintanilla. Their marriage registries report church dispensations (which we have not located) because of consanguinity in the fourth degree.

Nicolás and Beatriz had at least five children:

1. Nicolás (1676–1733). He married María Gertrudis de la Cerna in 1712 and had José Francisco, Nicolás, and a third child who died in infancy.
2. Ana Nicolasa (1678–1699). She married Bernabé de la Garza in January 1699. She died in December that same year, we believe related to childbirth.
3. Gregorio (1682–before 1741). He married María de Saldúa (1685–1756) in 1708 and had seven children.
4. Miguel (1685–1713). He never married and died at twenty-eight years of age.
5. Juan (1687–about 1750). His baptism godparents were Uncle Bartolomé and Aunt Nicolasa. He married first Catharina de Salazar in 1714 and, upon her death, María Sáenz in 1716.

Beatriz, age thirty-two, died as a result of childbirth when their youngest son, Juan, was born in 1687. Nicolás died a year later, also quite young at age thirty-three, and we think that their uncle Bartolomé and aunt Nicolasa raised their children. Bartolomé had a long life, during which he accumulated great wealth.

The christening priest registered Juan in his baptism record of April 20, 1687, as Juan de Quintanilla. Some accounts today would show him as Juan González Fernández. This has confused genealogists about both his ancestors and his descendants. We speculate that perhaps growing up with their cousins, the children of Nicolás and Beatriz chose to differentiate themselves by using Quintanilla instead of González as their surname.

We believe that the premature deaths of these children's parents resulted in a loss of wealth and social standing. They were raised as orphans and did not benefit from any wealth transfer that might have occurred had their parents lived a long life. And they certainly did not enjoy any of the social and economic privileges accorded to the founders and initial settlers. Juan's descendants did not recover until six generations later, in the mid-1800s.

Juan de Quintanilla first wed Catharina de Salazar on January 13, 1714. He was twenty-six, and she was twenty-four. Catharina resided in the valley of Huajuco and was the daughter of Capt. Pedro de Salazar and Inés Rodriguez de Montemayor. They got religious dispensation because they were second cousins. Juan's grandmother Beatriz Fernández and Catharina's grandmother Inés de la Garza[77] were sisters. The church granted dispensation for their marriage in August 1713, and witnesses included his cousin Bartolomé González de Quintanilla, Andrés de Tixerina (probably his uncle), and Sebastián Buentello. Another example of the continuing inbreeding at this time. They had one son together, Juan Ramón de Quintanilla,[78] born in September 1715. Catharina, however, died on September 9, 1715, probably related to the birth. Many genealogists stop here in terms of Juan's descendants.

The interesting fact is that Juan Ramon's baptism godparents were Diego Sáenz and his mother, Antonia de Saldívar. Antonia became Juan's mother-in-law and Diego his brother-in-law when he married Maria Sáenz a few months after his wife, Catharina, died. Why would he choose them? Antonia de Saldívar had married Miguel Sáenz in May 1680, and together they had at least six children: Agustina, Diego, Juan, Gertrudis, Nicolás, and Maria. They all lived in the valley of Huajuco, near Monterrey. Diego, born in 1683, was close in age to Juan, who was born in 1687. They were probably neighbors and close friends.

We think Juan has been the missing link in the Quintanilla ancestry line because genealogists have missed his second marriage. Once widowed, Juan married a second wife, María Gertrudis Sáenz, sixteen years old, when he was twenty-eight, on February 9, 1716. Life event records indicate that the Juan who married Catharina is the same Juan who married María Gertrudis. Both Juans lived in Valle del Huajuco (today Santiago), and the fact that María's mother was his firstborn's godmother is too much of a coincidence. We take all this as proof that these Juans were the same man. Juan and all his descendants use only the Quintanilla surname, following in the practice of his father, Nicolás.

Records also show ten children born to this couple (Juan Ramón was their half sibling):

1. Juan Diego (1717–1788), who married Antonia García in 1746 and had María, José Domingo, María Josefa, José Florencio, María Teodora, María Antonia, María Manuela, José Ygnacio, José Francisco, Luisa, and Christóbal.

77. Inés de la Garza Falcón married Capt. Diego Rodríguez de Montemayor, son of Capt. Miguel Montemayor del Canto and Mónica Rodríguez.

78. Juan Ramón went by the name Ramón only. In May 1746, he sought marriage dispensation from the dioceses to wed Catharina Soberón. They were third cousins, as their great-grandparents were siblings. Ramón's great-grandmother was Inés de la Garza Falcón, whose daughter was Inés Rodríguez, who in turn had Catharina de Salazar, Ramón's mother. Catharina Soberón's great-grandfather was Francisco de la Garza Falcón, whose son was Eugenio de la Garza Falcón, who in turn had Clara de la Garza Falcón, her mother. One of his witnesses was his stepuncle, Diego Sáenz. We ignore if the wedding took place, if he had any children with Catharina, or if he married again. Ramón and Catharina were both descendants of Blas de la Garza Falcón and Beatriz González Hidalgo in the fifth generation. We do not descend from Ramón.

2. María Josepha (1721), who married Francisco Javier de Padilla in 1739.
3. Juan (1723), who died in infancy.
4. Antonia Rosalía (1724), who married Joseph Jacinto Guerrero.
5. Gerónimo de Jesús (1727), who married María Olalla Gómez.
6. María Rita (1729), who married Juan M. Cárdenas in 1749.
7. Mathiana Gertrudis (1732), who married Joseph Mathías de San Miguel in 1757.
8. An unnamed child (1734), who died in infancy.
9. Ana María Petra (1735).
10. Ignacia Apolinaria (1740), who married Thomás de la Rosa.

It is unclear where Juan de Quintanilla died in 1759, at age seventy-two, but his burial mass occurred in Lampazos, Nuevo León, at the church of Nuestra Señora de los Dolores de la Punta de Lampazos. The record indicates that he lived with his wife, María Sáenz, in Santiago de Valladares, a mission that Spaniards founded in the late 1600s in neighboring Coahuila.

We ignore when or why they moved from the Valle del Huajuco. Santiago de Valladares is a very poor town in 2021, with only fifteen residents. It is in the county of Candela, Coahuila, and it borders with Lampazos, Nuevo León. It appears that whatever wealth his father, Nicolás, may have had, by the time Juan grew to adulthood, it had vanished, and he and Maria lived a life of poverty, as did their children. That is a common impact on a family when the breadwinner dies young. We have not found a death record for María, but she may not have lived long after Juan died. She probably moved in with one of their children as a widow.

Juan Diego, their eldest, married widow María Antonia García on August 8, 1746. He was twenty-nine years old; she was twenty-five. He needed to get a marriage dispensation from the church, which he filed in May 1746, just like his half brother Ramón had. He explained that his great-grandmother Beatriz González Hidalgo (de la Garza) was the sister of Luisa de la Garza, great-grandmother of Antonia García. Beatriz had María Beatriz Fernández de Tijerina, who in turn was the mother of his father, Juan de Quintanilla. On the other side, Luisa de la Garza was the mother of Juana Cadena and grandmother of Josepha Guajardo, Antonia's mother. The marriage record stated fourth-degree consanguinity (they were third cousins) and required they get dispensation for their marriage. He further stated that this blood relationship was unknown to them when they got engaged. José Diego and Antonia were both descendants of Blas de la Garza Falcón and Beatriz González Hidalgo in the fifth generation.

The marriage record lists María Antonia García as *"mulata libre"* (free mulatto). María Antonia had first married Christóbal García on August 3, 1738, when she was seventeen, but he died in 1742. The priest registered Christóbal as the illegitimate son of Pedro García Regalado, with no mother listed. Antonia García was baptized as María Antonia Margarita García Huajardo (it would be Guajardo today) on June 19, 1721, daughter of Esteban García and Josepha Huajardo, "*mestizos*" from Santa Catarina.[79]

Juan Diego and María Antonia had at least eleven children together:

1. Maria (1746).
2. José Domingo (1747). He married María Antonia Guerra about 1770–1771, daughter of Amador Guerra and Juana Francisca Rodríguez de Montemayor. Their children included José María, María Ygnacia, María Cayetana, María Zaragoza, Juan Joseph Rudecindo, José Antonio, José Cayetano, José Ylario, and Juana de Dios.
3. María Josefa (1749).
4. José Florencio (1751).
5. María Teodora (1753), who married José Luis Sánchez.
6. María Antonia (1755), who married José Cayetano Guerra in 1770.
7. María Manuela (1757), who married Santiago Fernández de Tijerina in 1781.
8. Twins José Francisco and José Ygnacio (1759). José Ygnacio married María Juana García in 1788.
9. Luisa (1761), who married Joaquín Fernández de Tijerina in 1785.
10. Christóbal (died in 1771).

Juan Diego and María Antonia named their youngest son after Maria Antonia's deceased first husband. Juan Diego died suddenly on March 31, 1788, in Monterrey. His unexpected death prevented a priest from performing the last rites. He was seventy years old. We suspect it was a heart attack. We have not found a death registry for Antonia, but we estimate that she may have died around 1801 at age seventy-nine.

Juan Diego and Antonia's second child was José Domingo, born on May 12, 1747, in Monterrey, Nuevo León. Because his mother had been classified as *mulata libre*, he, too, was classified as such. It is unclear why this was so. But all his children and grandchildren were then labeled as Spanish. Even more confusing.

He married María Antonia Guerra (1746–1810) sometime in 1770–1771, but we have not been able to locate the record. She was born on November 26, 1746, in Montemorelos, Nuevo León. Her parents were Amador Guerra and Juana Francisca Rodríguez de Montemayor. Records of their children's births begin in 1772 when they were both in their early twenties. Their first child was born in January 1772. José Domingo died between 1803 and 1806, according to the marriage records of his children. This was before María Antonia—she died on March 30, 1810, and she was a widow then. She was sixty-four years old.

79. If her parents were *mestizos*, it is unclear why she would be a "free mulatto."

José Domingo and Maria Antonia had at least nine children:

1. José María de Jesús (1772–1835), who married María Antonia González de Ochoa in Cadereyta in 1795. His great granddaughter Guadalupe Garza y Garza would marry his brother Juan Joseph Rudecindo's grandson Pedro Pablo Quintanilla in 1869.
2. María Ygnacia (1773–1828), who married Pedro José de Villarreal in 1803. Her father, Domingo, was still living.
3. María Cayetana (1775).
4. María Zaragoza (1776–1777).
5. Juan Joseph Rudecindo (1778–1835). He married Juana Rodríguez in 1801. His grandson Pedro Pablo Quintanilla would marry his brother Jose María's great-granddaughter Guadalupe Garza y Garza in 1869.
6. José Antonio (about 1780). He married Isabel Briseño in 1799 in Montemorelos. We have not located other records about him or a second marriage.
7. José Cayetano (1782). He married Maria Petra Charles in Ciudad Victoria in 1806, a place where he had been living since 1800. His father, Domingo, was deceased by then.
8. José Ylario (1783).
9. Juana de Dios (1786).

Our direct ancestor is Juan Joseph Rudecindo, their fifth child., but we also descend from his brother José María through his daughter María Guadalupe. He was born on March 2, 1778, in Monterrey. Juan Joseph married Juana Rodríguez on July 18, 1801; he was twenty-three, and she was sixteen. They had at least fourteen children, although only a few made it to adulthood, as several died in infancy:

1. Cayetano (1803–1864), who married Dorotea García Padilla (1817–1882). He was born on April 10, 1803. He was baptized José Dimas Calletano [*sic*] on April 30. Epistema Quintanilla, a granddaughter, married his sister María Trinidad's grandson Eulogio Garza.
2. José Guadalupe (1805–1808), who died in infancy.
3. Maria Trinidad (about 1806–1868), who married Ascencio Garza (1797–1870), son of José Antonio de la Garza and María Josefa Guajardo, in 1826. They had seven children. One grandson, Eulogio Garza, married older brother Cayetano's granddaughter Epistema Quintanilla.
4. Laureano (about 1808–1878), who married Eulalia Betancourt (1814–1899) in 1842. They lived in Ciudad Victoria, Tamaulipas. They had six children.
5. María Tiburcia (1809). We have found no more records other than her baptism. Therefore, we think she may have died in infancy.
6. Maria Guadalupe (1811–1811), who died in infancy.
7. José Andrés (1813–1813), who died in infancy.
8. José Vicente (1814–1814), who died in infancy.
9. José Domingo (1815–1840).
10. José Fermín (1818–1888). He first married María Concepción Montes (1827–1847) in 1841, with whom he had three children. After her death,

       he married Anastasia Garza (probably in 1847–1848), with whom he had eight more children.
11. José Antonio (1819–1903).
12. Another José Andrés (1821).
13. Juan Francisco (1823–1864). He married María de Jesús Garza.
14. María Antonia (1825–1875). Her mother was forty years old when she was born. She married Felipe de la Garza in 1841.

Juan died suddenly on August 28, 1835, at age fifty-seven. Juana died on April 16, 1850, at age sixty-four. Our Quintanilla line descends from Cayetano (1803–1864), their oldest son, who married Dorotea García Padilla (1817–1882) on November 25, 1835, only a few months after his father died. He was thirty-two years old and she was eighteen. Her parents were León García and Juana Padilla from neighboring Cadereyta.

Cayetano and Dorotea had the following children:

1. Pedro Pablo,[80] who was born in 1837, married María Guadalupe de la Garza-y-de la Garza. Her last name was later abbreviated to Garza y Garza. He died in 1906, at age sixty-eight, from arteriosclerosis. She died in 1910 at age fifty-nine of appendicitis.
2. María de los Angeles (1838), who never married.
3. Genoveva (1840), who married Cipriano Garza, the half brother to her sister-in-law Guadalupe Garza y Garza (siblings married siblings). Their children (Garza-Quintanilla) were Antonia (married Manuel Garza), Elvira (married Santos Perez), and León (married Amalia Rodríguez).
4. Maria Elena del Carmen (1843), who married Margarito Garza-Quintanilla and had SanJuana, Felipe, and Enrique Garza-Quintanilla. Carmen died young in 1878 (age thirty-three), and Margarito married again twice. He died by firearm at age seventy-two. Their son Enrique died from a fall from a moving train at age twenty-six. Their son Felipe also married three times after his first two wives died young.
5. Simón Judas Tadeo (1848), who married Ricarda Garza. Their children included Atilano, Petra, María, and Emigdia. He died a widower in 1922 at age seventy-three from angina.
6. María Manuela (1853), who married Nicolás Benavides (1856-1928). Their children included Guillermo, Eduardo, Nicolás, and Evangelina. She died in 1929.
7. Francisco (1858). He died one week old.
8. Tomás (1859). He died in 1860.
9. Josefa (1861). She was the youngest and never married. She died in 1928 at age sixty-six. Of note, her eldest brother, Pedro, was twenty-four years old when she was born.
10. José Guadalupe (1841–1907), who was Cayetano's illegitimate son. He always lived with Cayetano and his wife, Dorotea, but registries say that

80. There is a short biographical sketch on him in Agustin Basave, *Constructores de Monterrey* (Monterrey, NL: Editorial Instituto Tecnologico y de Estudios Superiores de Monterrey, 1945), 33–36.

Pedro Pablo Quintanilla-Garcia and Guadalupe Garza y Garza

he was a legitimate child of both. The family knew otherwise. José Guadalupe married Carmen González (1852–1944) in 1868. Their children included Cayetano, Juan, Jesús, Adolfo, Pedro, Benjamín, Rafael, María, Ana, and the twins Saúl and David.

Pedro Pablo[81] (1837–1906) married Guadalupe (Lupe) Garza y Garza (1850–1910),[82] daughter of Joaquín de la Garza-Cano and Maria Antonia de la Garza-Quintanilla, from Cadereyta, on January 9, 1869, at Monterrey's Cathedral. He was thirty-one, and she was eighteen, and his father and both her parents were deceased. They were related on the Quintanilla side. For instance, during their marriage bans, witnesses were Francisco Garcia Padilla (Pedro's uncle), Gregorio Garza (Lupe's first cousin), Francisco Garza Quintanilla (Pedro's second cousin and Lupe's uncle), and Cipriano Garza y Garza (Lupe's half brother).

We have found that both Pedro and Lupe were descendants of Bartolomé de Quintanilla and Juliana Farías from the 1500s through their daughters, Beatriz and Maria de Quintanilla. Lupe descended from Beatriz and her daughter Juana de Treviño, first cousin of Juliana de Quintanilla, while Pedro descended from Maria and her daughter Juliana.

Moreover, both Pedro and Lupe also descended from another prominent couple in Northern Mexico and South Texas, Blas de la Garza Falcón and Beatriz González Hidalgo.[83] Blas's father, Marcos Alonso Garza y Arcón, a

81. Ibid.

82. Guadalupe's real name was Guadalupe de la Garza de la Garza, which she probably shortened to Garza y Garza, a common practice at that time.

83. Clotilde P. García, *Captain Blas María de la Garza Falcón*.

Spanish nobleman, had married into the prominent Treviño family soon after his arrival in Mexico in the 1550s.

Blas arrived in Monterrey about 1605 and married Beatriz González Hidalgo. Among their many children, Francisco and Beatriz interest us. Francisco was an ancestor of Lupe Garza, while Beatriz was of Pedro P. Quintanilla. But an even closer relationship between both lineages came in the late 1700s. Pedro's grandfather Juan José Quintanilla and Lupe's great-grandfather José María Quintanilla were brothers (see the following chart). That made Pedro and Lupe second cousins once removed.

From a young age, Pedro Pablo developed an interest in manufacturing and innovation and became one of the most renowned local industrialists and

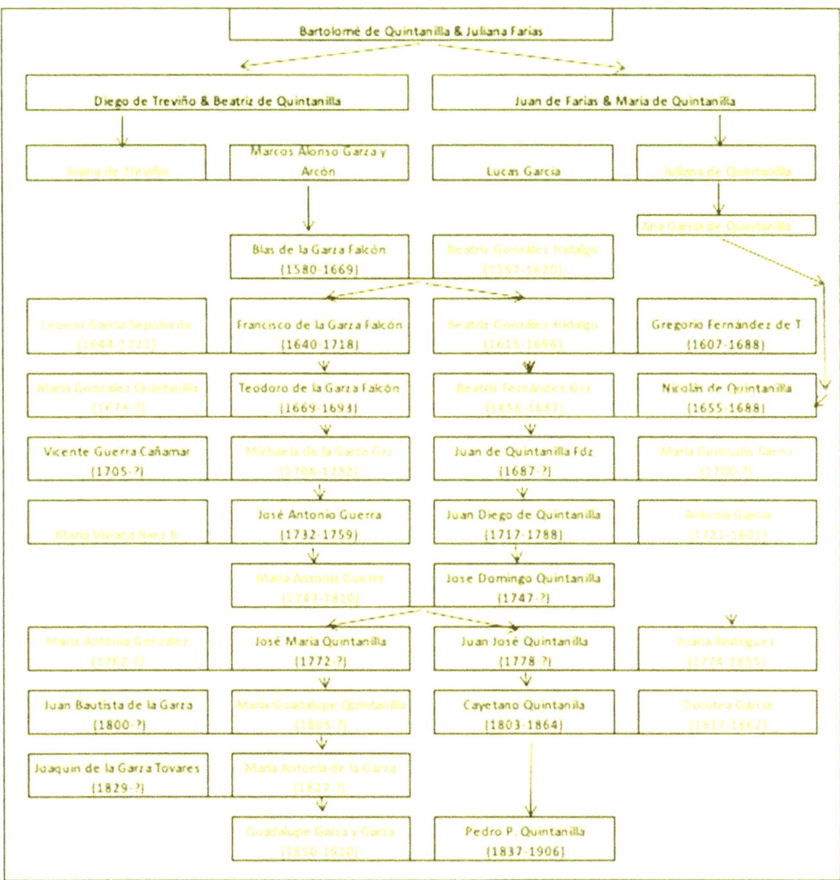

Green background = original settler
Blue background = common ancestor
Yellow background = unrelated ancestor
Blue font = male
Red font = female

entrepreneurs of his time. While his economic success was remarkable, his peers noted his unfaltering spirit and tenacity in developing different manufacturing enterprises. When he was a young man, he tripped and fell on a puddle of sodium hydroxide (caustic soda) that he used in the production of soap. He burned his cheeks and neck. He grew a beard to cover those scars after that incident.

Without a doubt, he took advantage of the economic boom Monterrey experienced from the 1870s to the early 1900s and became a true entrepreneur in the new economy. He started cultivating silkworms to promote the silk business in Mexico, for instance. He also had a match factory (La Constancia) and another one for gunpowder; he later started a factory for buttons and one for cornstarch (El Cisne). He loved music and played the clarinet, often with an orchestra at Teatro Progreso. He was very active in industrial expositions and won many awards, including a gold medal in the 1889 Paris World Fair, New Orleans in 1884, and New York in 1889—a total of eleven diplomas and medals. Some of these achievements are on display at El Obispado Museum in Monterrey.

Coming from a large family himself, Pedro Pablo and Lupe raised a big family as well. Together, they had the following children:

1. Pedro Cayetano was born on July 31, 1869, and christened a day later; he died a day later, on August 1. Recall Pedro and Lupe wed on January 9.
2. María Ysabel Epistema was born on November 11, 1870. She married Eulogio Garza-Vargas (1877–1956) in 1903. They were second cousins on the Quintanilla side: her grandfather and his grandmother were siblings. Their children were Eulogio (1906–1980), married to Guadalupe Calles, and Victoria (Vita) Garza-Quintanilla (1912–1992), who married Adolfo Eimbcke (1912–1979). She died in 1912, at age forty-one, leaving him a widower. He remarried to Elvira Treviño in 1914, with whom he had more children.

First row: Cayetano, Guadalupe Garza, Roberto, Pedro P. Quintanilla, Carlos
Second row: Gildardo; Maria and her husband, Santiago García-Ordóñez; Esther;
Joaquín; Epistema; and Galdino Monterrey, ca. 1900. Note: Guadalupe Garza was
blind and refused to have a full-face picture taken.

3. Maria Trinidad Gildardo was born on June 17, 1873. She remained single and died on June 5, 1925, at age fifty-one. She died of encephalitis lethargica, also known as sleeping sickness. According to news accounts from that time, there was an epidemic of encephalitis lethargica spreading around the world between 1915 and 1926. She was buried with her parents in Monterrey.

4. María Guadalupe (known as María) was born on January 18, 1875. She married Santiago García-Ordóñez (1870–1929) on March 10, 1894, the first of the children to wed. Their children included Santiago, Raquel, Pedro, Francisco, Oscar, Armando, Carlos, and Maria Guadalupe. She died on March 1, 1926, at age fifty-one, of breast cancer.

5. Maria Esther was born on September 21, 1876. She remained unmarried and died on August 8, 1925, at age forty-eight, nearly two months after her sister Gildardo's passing of meningeal tuberculosis. She was also buried with her parents.

6. Joaquín Benjamín was born on March 31, 1878. He died unmarried in Mexico City in 1916, at age thirty-eight, of epilepsy, and was buried with his parents in Monterrey.

7. Cayetano Florencio was born on February 23, 1880. He was a surgeon and settled in Mexico City with his wife, Consuelo Zamora, originally from Veracruz. They were married in 1914 in Jalapa, Veracruz. They did not have children. He died on July 16, 1961, at age eighty-one, of a heart attack.
8. Galdino Pablo was born on April 18, 1882. He studied law. He married Consuelo Coffin on February 1, 1912. He died on April 20, 1943, at age sixty-one, of aortic atheroma.
9. Carlos Juan was born on March 30, 1886. He was a surgeon. He married Ifigenia Castrellón (1892–1966) on November 29, 1918, in Durango. Their children included Ema, Carlos Jr., Joaquín, Josefina, Magda, Alicia, and Irma. He died in 1942, at age fifty-six, of bladder cancer, and his descendants live both in the US and in Mexico.
10. Roberto was born on January 5, 1890, and became a teacher. He first married Emilia Garza in 1917, but she died in childbirth, and so did the baby. He later married Florinda Sánchez (1887–1971) in 1921. Their children included Berta, Lucía, Elena, and Roberto Jr. The latter is the only one to have descendants. He died on January 9, 1964.

With at least two of these children (Esther and Joaquín), Pedro Pablo chose his friend Manuel Castillón as a witness for the birth registration. His son Galdino would eventually marry Manuel's granddaughter Consuelo Coffin, bringing together these two bloodlines.

Sadly, Lupe Garza went blind while experiencing "high fevers" when my grandfather, Galdino, was born. She remained legally blind until she died twenty-seven years later. Despite the great business success he enjoyed, Pedro Pablo was also keen on having his sons study a profession, since he had had no education himself. That was the downfall of his enterprises, because there was nobody to follow in his footsteps and take over the business when he passed away—only his daughters, who were not prepared for such endeavors, as they chose the education field. So, in the end, his businesses closed.